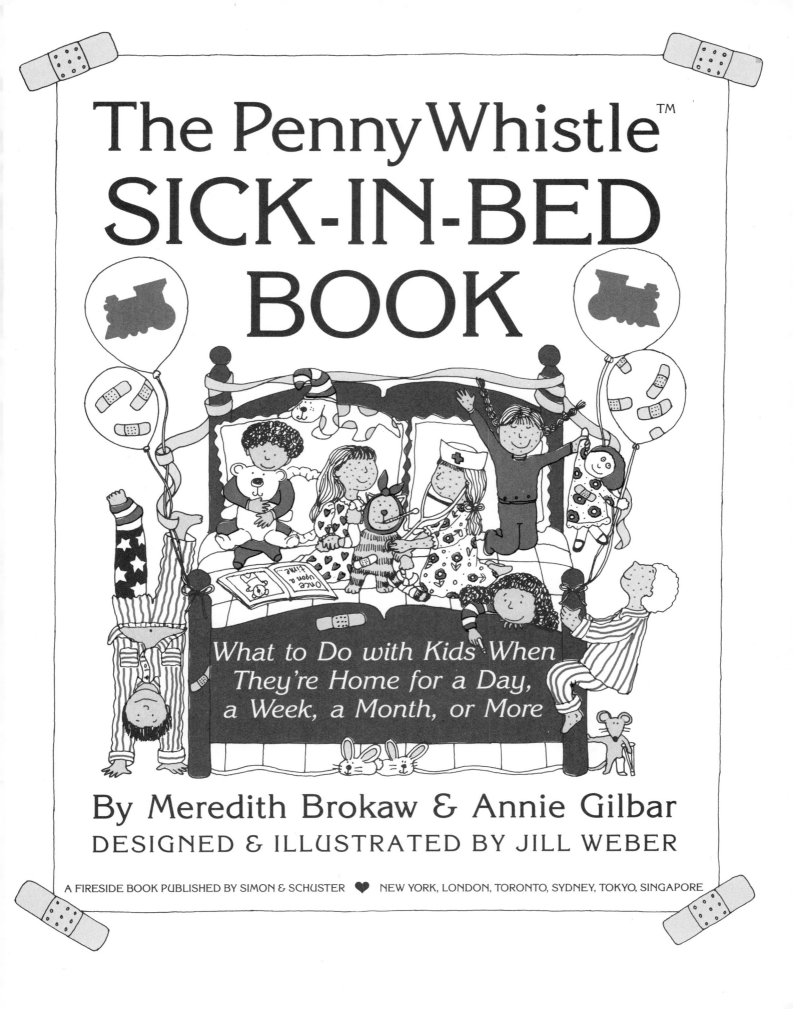

The PennyWhistle™
SICK-IN-BED
BOOK

What to Do with Kids When They're Home for a Day, a Week, a Month, or More

By Meredith Brokaw & Annie Gilbar
DESIGNED & ILLUSTRATED BY JILL WEBER

A FIRESIDE BOOK PUBLISHED BY SIMON & SCHUSTER ♥ NEW YORK, LONDON, TORONTO, SYDNEY, TOKYO, SINGAPORE

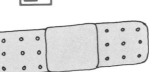

SIMON & SCHUSTER / FIRESIDE
Simon & Schuster Building
Rockefeller Center
1230 Avenue of the Americas
New York, New York 10020

Designed by JILL WEBER
Manufactured in the United States of America

10 9 8 7 6 5 4 3 2 1
10 9 8 7 6 5 4 3 2 1 PBK

Library of Congress Cataloging in Publication Data

Brokaw, Meredith.
   The Penny Whistle sick-in-bed book : what to do with kids when they're home for a day, a
week, a month, or more / by Meredith Brokaw & Annie Gilbar; designed & illustrated by Jill Weber.
      p.   cm.
   "A Fireside book."
   Includes index.
   ISBN 0-671-78690-3. — ISBN 0-671-78691-1 (pbk.)
   1. Creative activities and seatwork. 2. Games. 3. Sick children. I. Gilbar, Annie. II. Weber, Jill, ill.
III. Title.
GV1203.B685   1993   92-44300
649'.51—dc20   CIP

ISBN 0-671-78690-3
      0-671-78691-1 (PBK)

To Beth Yow,
our newest soul mate,
whose wise and careful work
is on every page

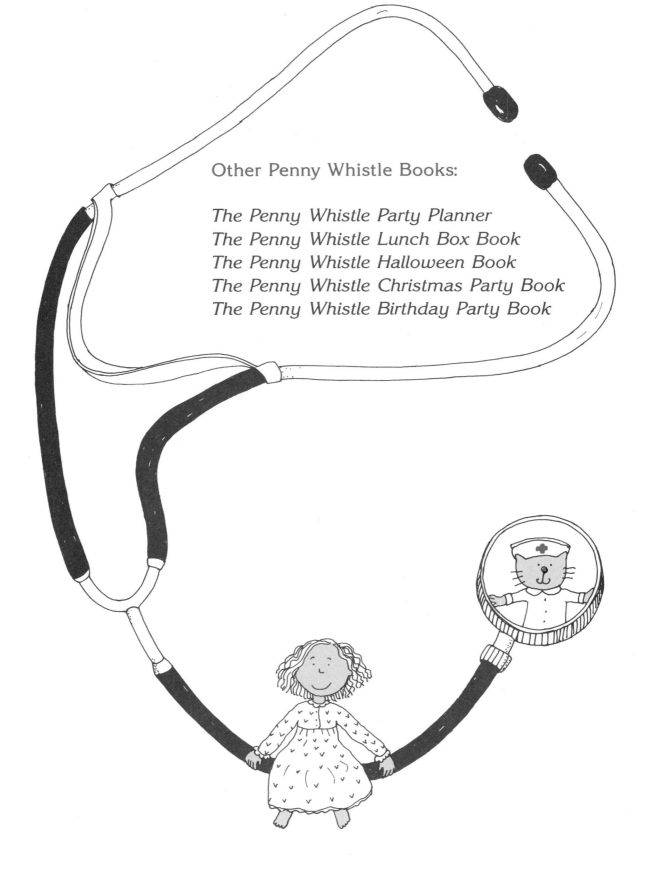

Other Penny Whistle Books:

The Penny Whistle Party Planner
The Penny Whistle Lunch Box Book
The Penny Whistle Halloween Book
The Penny Whistle Christmas Party Book
The Penny Whistle Birthday Party Book

ACKNOWLEDGMENTS

A special thank-you to Dr. Peter Waldstein for invaluable and confidence-building advice.

Scott Bennett
Jake Berman
Robert & Alec Bewkes
Jason, Rebecca & Ruth Bloom
Karen Borgie, ChildrensHospital L.A.
Iris Brooks
Jeff Buhai
Center for Early Education
Sarah Chapman
Susan Diamond
Ryan Donnelly
Don Ernstein, Wonderful Foods
Four Seasons Resort, Wailea
Inge & Sky Gilbar
Amy, Sybil & Zina Goldrich
Gabe, Mandy & Ronna Gordon
Michele Hèbert
Bobbie & Stacey Holston
Sarah & Sonia Israel
Jon Kasdan
Howie Kerpen
Jeremy Konner
Lois Levy

Jesse, Nancy & Zach Lynch
Rya & Jesse Lyons
Bill Miller
Sydny Miner
Christie & Morgan Mitchell
François Morrison
Northern Middle School, Dillsburg, PA
Vickie & Leslie Reynolds
Cory, Megan & Susie Russell
Jill Schiff
Judy Schunk
Amy & Kate Schwab
Andrew Schwartz
Barbara & Lew Schwartz
Jed & Wesley Schwartz
Garrett & Megan Smith
Hope Smith
Joanie Staigers
Annie, Joan & Nicholas Talarico
Evan & Joyce Bogart Trabulus
Laurie Waldstein
Laura, Michael & Sally Yow

And as always big and many thank-you's to our families—The Brokaws, The Gilbars and The Webers ♥

CONTENTS

WHEN YOUR CHILD GETS SICK / 11

PROJECTS & ACTIVITIES / 37

When Your ♥ Child ♥ Gets Sick

INTRODUCTION

More than likely, *sometime* during childhood your child will get sick and have to stay at home. It may be for just a day or two, when the cure for winter's sniffles is rest, chicken soup, and TV; or it may be for a week or so to recover from the ever-present flu bug, or the chicken pox epidemic sweeping the second grade. A broken leg or appendicitis can mean weeks of recovery; when a serious illness hits, weeks can become months.

For the child who is bedridden, and his concerned parents, even a day in bed can seem like an eternity. While sympathy and TLC are a great tonic, filling the hours for a child who doesn't feel well, has a shorter attention span than usual, and doesn't want to be where he is, isn't easy. No matter how good-humored the child, and how loving, caring, and clever the parents, both patience and ingenuity can quickly be sapped, leaving your child ready to look for new parents while you're prepared to throw away all of those well-meaning parenting skills and to try threats, tears, or even—yes—bribery. When Marc Gilbar was eight, he had what his doctor called "the worst case of chicken pox I have ever seen!" After two days of watching her poor pox-covered son try to maintain his normally cheerful disposition while she continually scrambled for "creative" and "absorbing" projects to keep him occupied (and herself from going crazy), Annie finally called her mother, who gave her the best advice ever: "Ask for help." So Annie called Marc's teacher, Iris Brooks, who came to the rescue not with a packet of homework but with a package of puzzles, word games, and suggestions for drawings she knew would challenge Marc and distract him from his misery. (Still, to this day, Annie swears that the package also contained magic dust from the healing fairy!)

When Sybil Goldrich's four-year-old daughter, Amy, came down with a case of nephritis (a kidney disorder, which in her case was symptomless and curable) the pediatrician said, "She'll be fine, but she has to stay *in bed*, twenty-four hours a day, for six weeks, and out of nursery school for six months." "I was speechless," remembers Sybil, "and absolutely terrified. I was confident Amy would recover physically but was overwhelmed by the prospect of filling what seemed like a lifetime of empty hours." Sybil started Amy's road to recovery when, in the guise of then president Lyndon Johnson, she presented Amy with a "Presidential Proclamation," which declared that "anybody in the United States of America with a sore kidney must stay in bed at all times." She then created a book of bed games just for Amy (which also came in handy a year later when her other daughter, Zina, needed eye surgery).

As three moms with six kids among us, we have been through many days at home with children who were not feeling up to par. *The Penny Whistle Sick-in-Bed Book* contains thoughts on dealing with the sick child, the importance of play and humor in the healing process, preparing for visits with the doctor, and, should it be necessary, going to the hospital. You'll also find a "Sick-Day

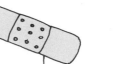

Box" full of surprises that can be opened only when your child is sick at home.

Naturally, in our research, we consulted the experts, including nutritionists, pediatricians, teachers, and, of course, other parents, many of whom had invaluable ideas for dealing with kids confined to bed. In fact, throughout the book you will find bits of advice from our pediatric adviser, Peter Waldstein, M.D., F.A.A.P., who has contributed much in the way of common sense, wisdom, and pragmatism from years of experience in treating hundreds of children. Although this is *not* a book of medical advice (more a collection of ways to make your child's—and your—experience of illness a little easier), you will find helpful hints for keeping your sick child comfortable as well as entertained.

We've also addressed the practical (and entertaining) side of things. For trips to the doctor's office or the hospital, we've designed two kits for you to put together that will help keep young children occupied in the waiting room and during their examination. You'll find chapters full of things to make and games to play—both for when your child is confined to his bed and for later when he's more mobile—and more activities than we hope you'll ever need (including ways of making your child's room a more pleasant, convenient environment). (Please note that whenever we say "you," we mean you, Mom, and/or you, Dad, and your child or children together.)

In addition, we've included some low-key exercises that may help your child's recovery and are fun to boot, as well as sections listing "books and videos to make him smile." Finally, there is a section on comfort foods that should tempt even the *most* reluctant eater.

And so, when the ten-hour day seems like a week, and your little angel is saying with increasing regularity, "Mom, I'm *bored*" (and you've already gone through all the board games in the closet, and soap operas don't seem like the appropriate alternative), take a slow, deep breath, and open *The Penny Whistle Sick-in-Bed Book*. We've got some ideas to save the day.

♥ *A lovely poem from* A Child's Garden of Verses, *by Robert Louis Stevenson, called "The Land of Counterpane" describes a child's feelings about being sick.*

When I was sick and lay a-bed,
I had two pillows at my head,
And all my toys beside me lay
To keep me happy all the day.
And sometimes for an hour or so
I watched my leaden soldiers go,
With different uniforms and
*   drills,*
Among the bed-clothes, through
*   the hills;*
And sometimes sent my ships in
*   fleets*
All up and down among the
*   sheets;*
Or brought my trees and houses
*   out,*
And planted cities all about.
I was the giant great and still
That sits upon the pillow-hill,
And sees before him, dale and
*   plain,*
The pleasant land of
*   counterpane.*

WHEN YOUR CHILD GETS SICK

A tip from Laurie Waldstein (Dr. Waldstein's wife): Before giving your child medicine, put an ice cube on his tongue. It will deaden his taste buds.

Also from Laurie Waldstein: "To stop tears in a little kid, tell him you will try to collect his tears in a bottle to save because they are so precious."

"A child doesn't stop being a child just because he is sick," says Dr. Peter Waldstein. When your child is ill, he needs not only the medication your doctor prescribes but also the emotional support and encouragement of his family.

Children's reactions to being sick vary with the individual, but there are similarities. With the onset of an illness, no matter how minor, a child may become quiet and withdrawn. This stage usually passes quickly, and your child may become angry, wondering why he got sick and feeling frustrated because his illness is something he can't control.

"You as a parent are a crucial factor in determining whether your child's emotions and behavior will be beneficial or detrimental to his treatment and recovery," explains Dr. Waldstein. "If you are anxious and fearful, your child will immediately pick up on that and this will make your child more anxious as well." Parents need to know that they play an important role in their child's well-being. Dr. Waldstein emphasizes, "They need to know what they can do to help their child's physical and emotional needs, and how important emotional stability is for their child's psychological well-being. I always encourage parents to help their children by allowing them to show their fears and concerns. They should try to clarify misconceptions while showing a clear understanding of, and sympathy for, such fears."

Put yourself in your child's place. Remember when you were young and didn't feel so hot. The most reassuring parents are the moms and dads who say, "Don't worry. The doctor is going to take care of you, and so are we. Everything will be fine." This doesn't mean lying to your child. In fact, Dr. Waldstein is emphatic about parents' telling their children the truth. Vicki Reynolds remembers the time her daughter Leslie slashed her chin open on the side of a neighbor's pool when she was seven. Leslie held her chin together as Vicki drove her to the doctor's office. Vicki was concerned that Leslie was in a lot of pain, but all Leslie could talk about was her fear that she would get a shot. "A shot!" said Vicki. "You never get a shot in your chin." However, the first thing the doctor did when he saw Leslie was give her a shot of novocaine right in the chin to deaden the pain before stitching up the wound. Remembers Leslie today, "It took me a while to trust my mom again."

The lesson? "If your child is going to get a shot, tell him," advises Dr. Waldstein. "I always tell my patients if an injection will hurt them (not a week before, to allow them to build up their anxiety, but *just* before). If your child handles the situation bravely, tell him so; your praise will enhance his self-esteem and will help him deal with the next similar situation. If he cries, tell him that it's perfectly fine to cry—that crying is a natural reaction to an unpleasant situation. No matter which reaction your child has he will remember that you were honest with him and he will continue to trust you."

You cannot kiss, hug, or reassure your child too much when he is not feeling well. Any encouragement will comfort your child, help him in his recovery, and make the time at home more pleasant. "You can't spoil a sick child," says Dr. Waldstein. This *doesn't* mean that your child suddenly gets to make the rules, or that inappropriate or unacceptable behavior will be tolerated. Parents can let a child make certain rules (posting a sign on the patient's door to "please knock" before entering, for example) that will increase the child's feelings of identity and control. Lisa Gilbar's favorite version of this, which she uses even for the slightest aches and pains, is "Anyone who enters this room must be smiling!"

♥

Jill's favorite memory of when she and her brothers were sick was being able to be in her mom's bed. The combination of special foods, the large bed, the TV at whim, and the attention sometimes made it worth getting sick.

ANYONE WHO ENTERS THIS ROOM MUST BE SMILING

THE IMPORTANCE OF PLAY

To help your young child in a cast get around the house, use an old-fashioned red wagon!

The importance of play in a child's recovery from illness cannot be overstated. It is widely recognized that play is an essential part of a child's emotional and psychological development; play brings pleasure to a child, and such a feeling of happiness is crucial to getting well.

Moreover, "play can benefit the parent as well as the child," explains Dr. Waldstein. Utilizing laughter as a tool while you are taking care of your sick child decreases tension; finding the humor in situations, making jokes (while never making light of his feelings), and acting silly may help everyone feel better.

Play also gives your child a feeling of control over his life and environment. "Children can't control being sick," says Dr. Waldstein. "Play gives your child the opportunity to feel joy and satisfaction. It takes a passive situation—being sick in bed—and transforms it into enjoyable activity." Play is one of the few experiences in which a child can take charge. It need not be goal-oriented or competitive to be beneficial (although a competitive child gains great pleasure from excelling and winning in play, even when he is sick). Just by planning, communicating, making decisions, physically manipulating, and creating during play, your child gains self-confidence and feels more in control of his environment. This lift in spirits speeds up the recovery process. In fact, a sense of humor, creativity, and a positive attitude have been found to be important factors in overcoming illness. "At any rate, long before my own serious illness, I became convinced that creativity, the will to live, hope, faith and love. . .contribute strongly to healing and to well-being. The positive emotions are life-giving experiences," says Norman Cousins, in his book *Anatomy of an Illness as Perceived by the Patient: Reflections on Healing and Regeneration.*

Play is also one of the most effective ways of communicating. Play is extremely important for a child because he does not have the same command of the language as an adult; it is more difficult for him to express himself verbally, particularly when his feelings are negative or angry or when he is not feeling well and is also scared. Young children, especially, tell us about themselves through play. You can use play to rehearse a visit to the doctor's office and to practice different ways of dealing with the stressful situation. Through play a child can learn what a specific procedure will involve, how he can participate, and how he is expected to cooperate. He can express his fears and anxieties and there is time for you to reassure him and to clarify any misconceptions he may have. A child who is relaxed both through the confidence he has gained from his parents and through play is generally more cooperative and is in a better physical state to receive and benefit from treatment. "Play is an activity that should be prescribed more than antibiotics—a self-healing activity that releases tension and makes a child happier," explains Dr. Waldstein. And isn't that what every parent wants?

Playmobil has wonderful toys that are hospital related including Hospital Ward, Hospital Operating Room, Ambulance, Paramedic, Rescue Copter, and First Aid Tent.

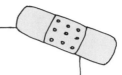

THE BEDRIDDEN CHILD

When your child is sick there will probably be a period when he should stay in bed, whether it's the first couple of days of the flu, resting after a broken arm, or the early stages of a longer illness. Unfortunately, the necessity of staying still is one of the most difficult concepts to explain to a child; convincing your sick one to stay in bed or simply to slow down can be frustrating and even, at times, impossible.

Having to stay in bed may also alter your child's perception of time. It is common for a child in bed to feel as if he were constantly in a state of waiting; time seems to drag on forever. Such a state of mind is more than boredom—your child becomes frustrated and anxious, often out of proportion to the actual situation.

When Jeff Buhai was thirteen he suffered a slipped disk. The injury was so serious that he had surgery (a laminectomy) the very next week and ended up in a full-body cast. He recuperated at home in a hospital bed for nearly ten months. "That's a long time for anyone—for me it seemed like a lifetime," Jeff recalls. But this immobility encouraged Jeff to take the initiative to try to do things he never did before, like reading the newspaper every day, learning how to play chess (he even played chess by mail), and ordering small items from catalogs so the mailman would often bring a surprise. "I guess it made me stronger," says Jeff today, "but if you want to know the truth, I think it made me a nerd. I spent the entire seventh grade in bed, so I missed out on all the socializing that was going on." That must be why Jeff wrote one of his most famous screenplays, *Revenge of the Nerds*.

Keep in mind that the immobile child thinks of himself as a kind of prisoner, even if he's only resting in bed for a few days. Remember that physical activities help form a child's self-image and feelings of strength and accomplishment. If a child's mobility must be restricted over a long period of time, it can threaten a child's sense of self.

♥

Sarah Chapman's son Scott Bennett broke his leg and was bedridden. So she gave him a bell to ring when he needed her. When his friends came to visit he loved showing off by ringing for his mom.

♥

If your child is in bed for a long time, try giving him a special back rub or foot massage.

♥

For the child confined to bed, the bed itself can be an ever-changing environment. With a simple clothesline and a sheet, it can be a tent, a cave, or a sailboat.

♥

If possible, why not persuade a favorite barber or hair-dresser to bring a little fun by treating your child to a haircut or a new hairdo at home? If you've got a daughter (especially a teenager), a professional manicure (or pedicure!) will really be a treat.

"It is important," explains Dr. Waldstein, "to understand that a child who is physically restricted, even for a day or two, is out of touch with the world and his friends. If the child is not distracted by being given something to occupy his mind and his hands, he will often begin to focus attention on his illness and on his body."

So what do we do? It's actually pretty simple. The child who has little chance to experience his normal environment must have that environment brought to him. Games and activities that he can do while he's in bed will reduce his sense of physical and social isolation.

Some tips on dealing with the immobile child follow:

★ Whether your child is in bed or in a wheelchair, it can take time to arouse his interest and enthusiasm. Don't be discouraged—just try a little harder to engage him in games and activities.

★ It is important to give your child confidence and to help him find pleasure in learning what he can do, not to focus on what he cannot do.

★ "You may find that an immobile child who also doesn't feel well may suddenly want to participate in games or activities that would at other times be below his age," says Dr. Waldstein. A child who is a whiz at chess when he is well may suddenly be perfectly happy playing memory or connect the dots.

★ If your child likes to watch television programs or videos, encourage him to watch those that will make him laugh (see page 119).

★ Your child's attention span may be shorter than usual. Be prepared for this by providing him with alternative games and activities so he won't become impatient or frustrated.

★ Dr. Waldstein advises: "Children who are physically restricted for any period of time can let out their anger and feel a sense of control through particular games. Your child may show particular glee when he pounds pegs into a board or hammers logs together. Activities like these allow him to let out his anger and pent-up energy."

★ The immobile child may take special pleasure in assembling mobiles or model airplanes and playing with yo-yos and other string toys.

★ Encourage your child to play games that make him feel strong. Show him how to use weights and perform other strength-building exercises (see page 26).

★ Many sick children respond well to schedules. If you set up a regular daily routine for the child who loves organization, he will enjoy knowing what's coming next and even marking off the things he's doing on a daily chart. Jeff Buhai explains: "In all that time in bed I loved being in control of what my day would be like. If I watched television, I had to do my homework during the commercials. At a certain time my school tutor would come over. Another time was set aside to write letters to my pen pals. After three o'clock I was able to call my friends who were home from school."

DEALING WITH HOMEWORK

When one of the concerns parents have is that their sick child will fall behind in his schoolwork, Lois Levy, of the Center for Early Education (CEE) in Los Angeles, California, suggests the following:

★ Don't make homework an issue or a worry. Getting your child well is your main consideration. When he is better, you can give him a little work at a time.

★ If your child is out for a day or so, a friend or a sibling can bring homework to him. This will give your child the extra treat of seeing a friend.

★ Call the school ahead of time and, if necessary, make arrangements to pick up the homework assignments personally.

★ Sometimes when a child has been absent from school, the parents want him to make up everything that he has missed. This is impossible—particularly if the child is not feeling well. Instead, have your child concentrate on core assignments so he won't be behind when he returns to class. The other work does not have the immediacy and can be made up when your child returns to school. Sometimes too much is too much.

★ Look beyond homework to skills your child can tackle. Use art projects, games, and computers to make learning more exciting.

★ Some schools and libraries will loan games, books, even computers and their programs, to children who can't be in school. They will also make suggestions to parents as to what items to purchase that will be both fun and beneficial.

♥
Jill had a bunch of trays set up for Remy when he was sick. One had the ongoing Lego project, another a jigsaw puzzle, another some craft project. Every so often she would intersperse these trays with a tray of homework.

DEALING WITH VISITORS

In Jill's neighborhood, the first child to contract the chicken pox would play with all the other children so they could itch together.

If your child is not contagious but will need to spend more than a week in bed, try throwing him a party. Use any of the ideas from The Penny Whistle Party Planner *or* The Penny Whistle Birthday Party Book, *or even our Christmas or Halloween book. You will find that celebrating your child's recuperation with a real party will be fun and unforgettable for everyone.*

Dealing with visitors when your child is ill just takes plain common sense. Obviously, when a child is at the beginning of his illness, he will not want to see anyone, nor should he have to. It is generally not a good idea to allow visitors at such a time, whether they are adults or children (this applies whether or not your child has a communicable disease). As your child gets better (he has no fever, he's become more mobile, and he is truly on the road to recovery), visitors are often a good idea. Particularly for the recuperating child and for the child who has a long-term, noncommunicable illness, visitors provide a welcome change of pace and help speed the recovery process.

★ Any time your child is sick at home, visitors by phone will be most welcome. Encourage relatives, friends, and schoolmates to call to tell him jokes and bring him news of the outside world to lessen his feelings of isolation.

★ Another easy way to bring the outside world in is to ask friends to make cards or drawings and drop them off or mail them.

★ Always check with your child before you invite his friends to visit.

★ Ask your child's prospective visitors to phone before dropping by.

★ It's a good idea to set limits for both the number of visitors and the length of time they visit.

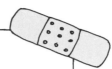

THE DOCTOR'S OFFICE

A visit to the doctor's office can be traumatic for a child, particularly when he is not feeling well. Here are some suggestions for keeping his fear and anxiety to a minimum while enhancing his feelings of security and confidence when visiting the doctor.

★ Take your child for regular checkups. Visiting the doctor's office when he is well will decrease his fear of visits when he is ill. He will know the personnel, the equipment, and especially his doctor.

★ Bring some familiar things (books, toys, one of your child's favorite "snugglies" or comfort objects) and your "Waiting Room Kit" (see page 22) to the doctor's office with you.

★ Call your pediatrician not only for prescriptions but also for advice and reassurance. (If your doctor is too busy to talk to you on the phone, get another doctor!) Let your child develop his own relationship with his doctor. Dr. Waldstein often answers his own phone and asks to speak to the child if the child is old enough to verbalize his feelings and describe his symptoms.

★ Kids are intuitive. If you are anxious about bringing your child to the doctor's office, he will pick up on these feelings. Relax as much as you can. Show confidence that you and your doctor will deal with your child and his illness.

★ Ask your doctor what you can do for your child when he is sick. Parents are an important part of the healing process.

★ Always tell your child the truth. If you treat your child with respect and honesty, he will learn to trust you and the doctor. "Children experience less distress when they know how a procedure will feel than when they only know what will happen," explains Dr. Waldstein.

★ Take your child with you when you see *your* own doctor. Dr. Waldstein believes that it is helpful for your child to see that adults, too, visit the doctor. He doesn't have to see the examination; even sitting in the waiting room will allow him to see that there is nothing to fear from medical environments.

★ Encourage your child to playact, even when he visits the doctor's office. Dramatic play is a natural activity for young children and if you can enter their imaginary world with them, you will see how they really feel.

★ "Children's imaginations, especially those of preschoolers, are so vivid that the child may believe a medical procedure is some kind of punishment for an unrelated event," explains Dr. Waldstein. "Allowing children to participate in a procedure makes them feel independent. Giving them some choices ('Would you like this on your left arm or the right one?' 'Would you like to have your blood drawn first, or would you like to weigh yourself before we start?') also makes them feel that they have some power over the situation."

Take a crayon or a washable marker for making pictures on the big sheet of white paper that covers the examining table.

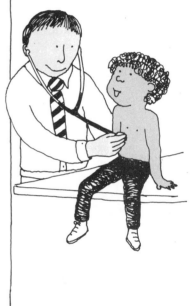

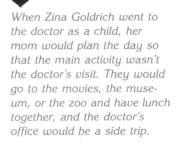

When Zina Goldrich went to the doctor as a child, her mom would plan the day so that the main activity wasn't the doctor's visit. They would go to the movies, the museum, or the zoo and have lunch together, and the doctor's office would be a side trip.

THE WAITING ROOM KIT

♥

Make a notebook of all the "paper games" found in the "Games" section (see pages 81–106) to put in your "Waiting Room Kit."

♥

Your child can create a drawing for the doctor while he waits. Dr. Waldstein hangs his up in the waiting room!

♥

Etch A Sketch (Ohio Art) is great for waiting rooms and while your child is in bed.

Waiting takes a toll on both you and your child. Our "Waiting Room Kit" is a bag full of creative activities and objects that will keep your youngster busy and happy during such times. The allure of the kit for your child is that it contains things that he plays with or uses *only* while waiting at the doctor's office or the hospital. (You might even be able to use these games and activities to distract your child if he had to undergo long or unpleasant tests and procedures.)

Get a small backpack. Let your child decorate his special bag with felt-tip pens or fabric paint. The following list will give you some ideas for the contents of your child's bag (you can gift wrap all or some of the items, if you like). If your child will be making frequent visits to the doctor during a prolonged illness, rotate the items regularly to keep his interest. Ask your child for his own ideas to add to the list.

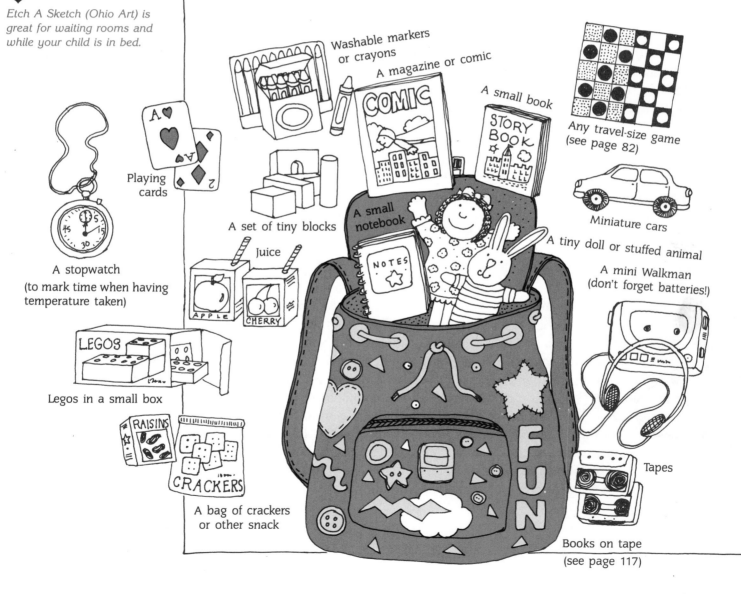

Washable markers or crayons

A magazine or comic

A small book

Any travel-size game (see page 82)

Playing cards

A set of tiny blocks

Juice

A small notebook

A tiny doll or stuffed animal

Miniature cars

A mini Walkman (don't forget batteries!)

A stopwatch (to mark time when having temperature taken)

Legos in a small box

A bag of crackers or other snack

Tapes

Books on tape (see page 117)

THE DOCTOR'S BAG

A way of making your young child feel like part of the "visit the doctor" process is to have him bring along his own "Doctor's Bag" whenever he visits the doctor's office. This lets him act out or play "doctor" while he's in the waiting room. To lessen the tension of the visit, some doctors even let the child use his play instruments while he's being examined.

The Doctor's Bag can be put together from items purchased at the drugstore. It can be stocked with a generous amount of disposable supplies such as tape, Band-Aids, elastic bandages, face masks, paper hats, tongue depressors, Q-tips, cotton balls—all useful props for medical dramatics. For your child to complete his examinations, include a doll or a stuffed animal, "hospital" clothing, and a blanket.

Beth and Laura Yow always played with items from their own doctor's bags whenever they visited their doctor, Dr. Steven Robbins, in Media, Pennsylvania. But their bags were extra special: Their dad also was a doctor and he filled up their play bags with old, but real, medical instruments and accessories. "It was the perfect way to keep the girls occupied, while at the same time keeping their minds off the doctor's examination," says their father.

PARENT CONSENT FORM ... FOR MEDICAL CARE

♥
When Remy Weber visited his grandmother he cut his foot and needed to get stitches. Suddenly Remy's grandmother found that the doctors would not treat Remy without Jill's permission. Be sure when your kids are traveling to visit someone—even family—that you send a signed and notarized authorization form for medical treatment (see form on page 157).

24

THE HOSPITAL

Whether it is for overnight observation before a minor surgical procedure or for major surgery and a more extended stay, checking into the hospital can be an upsetting experience for the child and the parents alike. We hope the following tips will make things a little easier for all of you.

Preoperative information should provide the child with certain essential facts about his impending surgery, including what will happen to him and what will be expected of him. The child should also be assured that he is not being punished for his injury or illness and that no other body part will be harmed.

Dr. Waldstein offers the following tips for coping with the hospital stay:

★ Doctors have found that older children (seven to twelve years of age) seem to benefit when they are prepared for their upcoming surgery one week before admittance to the hospital, while younger children (four to seven years of age) are better off when they are prepared the night before surgery. Older children seem to be able to digest the information and go about their daily lives; younger children tend to worry and, when presented with more time to worry, let their imaginations get out of hand. But there are also other younger children who just forget the information if it is given to them too far ahead of time. In either case, it is best to prepare your young child the night before. (This, of course, does not rule out a hospital visit to familiarize your child with the personnel and the equipment, which can be done a week before.)

★ Give your child as much information as you think he will understand at his age. "In the absence of accurate information," explains Dr. Waldstein, "children of all ages often develop fantastic and distorted ideas." Facts provide a framework for the child to use in trying to assess what could potentially be a frightening and disturbing experience. With truth as their weapon, even very young children can visualize what is going to happen. Through the process of imagination, they can "rehearse," and thus prepare themselves for their stay in the hospital. (This is also true for children who recover at home.)

★ Talk to the doctors and to the administrators. Ask any questions you want. Do not be intimidated! Your confidence in asking will give that same confidence to your child. Try to keep your fears and anxieties to yourself, or your child will become fearful, too.

★ Remember that, as a parent, you are "the keeper of the positive attitude" — a role not to be underestimated!

★ Ask your doctor to help you arrange at least one trip to the hospital beforehand. (Many hospitals have special preadmission programs for children.) Meet some nurses, see the rooms and the beds, ride in a wheelchair, and ask a doctor if you can try on a mask. You can meet the orderlies in their greens. This will familiarize your child with the uniforms. Ask to let your child see and, if possible, "try out" any equipment he might use later. Allow a toddler to play with the hospital equipment with an adult. This will decrease his anxiety about

If a child is stuck in the hospital, bed covers and pillows from home are a huge comfort.

the strangeness of this environment and increase a sense of familiarity and control that is essential to keeping him as calm and cooperative as possible.

★ Ask your doctor to introduce your child to another child who has had the same condition or procedure. Says Sybil Goldrich, "When Zina needed her eye surgery, we introduced her to another little girl who also wore an eye patch for a while. Zina tried hers on and was prepared for what it felt like and what she would look like when it was her turn."

★ Play, says Dr. Waldstein, is extremely useful when you want the child to cooperate during treatments and procedures that are threatening to him. So don't feel that nurses are being silly or insensitive when they are being playful with a child who is ill. You will also often find a nurse doing the same thing again and again with your child. "Repetition through play lets your child practice dealing with the environment in an active, rather than a passive, manner," explains Dr. Waldstein. In a hospital setting, you will often see children pretending to be nurses or doctors "treating" stuffed animals or dolls. Sessions where the children "play hospital," or "doctor," or "nurse" (using equipment like stethoscopes, flashlights, tongue depressors, bandages, masks, surgical gloves, even syringes and suture-removal kits) familiarize your child with this special equipment and make him more comfortable when he is around it. Sybil Goldrich says, "We spent a day in the hospital and let Zina play with the equipment and even let a nurse bandage her eyes. By the time the surgery came, she was comfortable with all that was going on around her. And by the time the next surgery came, she was a fearless expert." Remembers Howie Kerpen, "When I was ten I hurt a disk in my back and had to go to the hospital. What I remember most is a nurse named Gina who lay down next to me (on what I think was a gurney) and pretended that she couldn't move, too. She showed me what she *could* do, like clap her hands and move herself up and down on the gurney. And she showed me how to make the funniest faces. Her pretending with me made me feel absolutely wonderful. I still remember her today, almost thirty years later."

★ A hospital can be a threatening place even for adults. Respect your child's need to express himself, to explore his new and foreign environment, and to play—both for pleasure and as a means of coping. Try to keep in mind that during this time your child needs your understanding and support more than ever. If he expresses a fear, try to allay it; if he interrupts with a question you may have already answered, answer it again patiently. A little leeway and a lot of kisses will go a long way and will always be remembered.

★ Often the parent or the care giver can sleep in the child's room in the hospital. Find out how available you can be to your child and how involved you can be in his care.

♥ As a little girl, Zina Goldrich had to stay in the hospital. She still remembers her mom and dad "camped out" in her room with her.

♥ Meredith's dad was a doctor and often had one of his five children accompany him on his hospital rounds.

Whenever you breathe in an exercise, pretend you are a balloon: Breathe in as you expand your stomach and chest muscles on all sides; then exhale as you contract them.

When your child is sick, exercise should not be a chore. Exercise is another activity a child can do that will help him feel that he has control over his body. Using his body should be an enjoyable and fun activity that allows the child to feel that he is helping himself get better.

The following exercises are not too vigorous but will promote flexibility, circulation, and proper breathing (breathing draws energy into the body; peaceful, even breathing keeps the system and thoughts calm). Stretching muscles that are tight from sitting in bed can help your child in recovering from an illness and will aid in preventing injury when he resumes his normal activity. Your child may also find exercise to be a means of relieving stress, depending on his condition or illness.

The exercises in this section are suitable for children of all ages. However, it is important to note that as younger and older children may perceive their bodies and illnesses differently, your approach to exercise must be appropriate for your child's level of understanding. Older children can comprehend how exercise benefits the body and the mind. Your younger child will respond better to suggestions about exercise if you make exercise more of a game. Also, remember to allow your child a range of exercise options from which he may choose. We suggest that you consult with your doctor before undertaking any exercise program.

The first six exercises were recommended by Michele Hèbert, an exercise specialist in La Jolla, California. They are based on simple yoga postures.

Spinal Stretch

This exercise stretches your back and may be done in bed or on the floor. Lie on your back with your arms at your sides. As you breathe in deeply through your nose, bring your arms up toward the ceiling and back behind your head, stretching your body as you raise your arms up and down. Exhale vigorously through your lips as you bring your arms back to the sides of your body. Repeat three times.

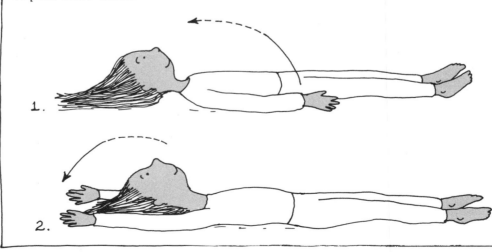

Knees-to-Chest Ball

This exercise stretches and massages your back and is best done on the floor. Hug your knees to your chest and wrap your arms around your knees. Rock from side to side, breathing in to one side and out to the other. Repeat three times.

Bridge

This exercise works your back and lower body and may be done in bed or on the floor. Lying on your back, bend your knees, bringing your feet close to your hips. As you breathe in, bring your hips high to the ceiling so your body is making a bridge. Hold the position for a count of five to ten, depending on your strength, breathing comfortably. Slowly lower your hips as you exhale. Repeat three times.

♥

Squeeze sponge balls in your hand. You can also squeeze a sponge ball between your knees while lying on your back.

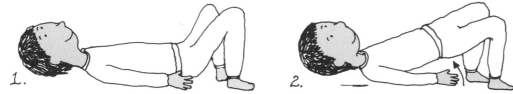

Dog and Cat Stretch

This exercise stretches your entire body and is best done on the floor. Get on your hands and knees. As you inhale, flatten your spine and bring you head up and back (as a dog would stretch). As you exhale, round your spine and bring your chin to your chest (as a cat would stretch). Repeat three times.

♥

Playing balloon "volleyball" is great exercise.

Cobra Pose

This exercise stretches your upper body and may be done in bed or on the floor. Lie face down and place your palms under your shoulders. As you breathe in, raise your head, chest, and spine up slowly, like a snake. Hold it for a count of five to ten, breathing calmly. Lower yourself slowly. Repeat three times.

Nancy Lynch taught her son Zach creative visualization when he couldn't sleep. She had him close his eyes and think about his breathing. Then she asked him to imagine that with each breath in he was growing as light as a feather, like a balloon floating away or an astronaut weightless in space. Then she had him imagine that with each breath out he was getting heavier until he felt as though he were sinking into his bed. By this time Zach would usually be fast asleep.

Fingers or toes peeking out of a cast can really benefit from this exercise.

Creative Visualization

This exercise uses your imagination to help you see yourself getting better. Lie on your back in bed or on the floor. Take a deep breath and as you breathe out feel your body go limp all over.

Gently close your eyes. Think of things that make you laugh. Imagine yourself playing with friends. Feel yourself healthy and well and filled with energy.

Now think of your breath. Feel the breath going into your body through your nostrils and filling you with lightness. Feel the breath leave through your nostrils and let go of any heaviness. Feel yourself becoming lighter and lighter with each breath.

The following exercises were put together by Nancy Lynch, fitness director of Hampshire Hills Sports and Fitness Club in Milford, New Hampshire. They were designed for young children but anyone can benefit from doing them.

Reach for the Stars

This exercise works your shoulders and is a good overall stretch. It may be done while seated in bed or standing on the floor. Stretch for the sky with one arm and "grab a star"; then reach with the other arm. This can also be done with both arms raised high overhead. If you sway like a tree from side to side, you will stretch the obliques (the muscles on the sides of your body). Repeat three times.

Hello, Good-bye

This ballet warm-up exercise stretches different parts of the body, and may be done in bed or on the floor. Put your legs straight out in front of you. Say, "Hello, toes," and flex your toes toward you or the ceiling. Then say, "Good-bye, toes," and point your toes away from you or the ceiling. Now do this with your fingers. Put your arms straight out in front of you. Say, "Hello, fingers," and flex your fingers straight up. Then say, "Good-bye, fingers," and flex your fingers down. Repeat three times.

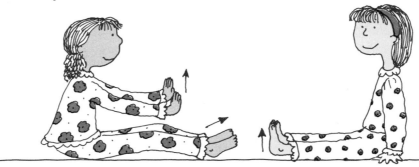

I Don't Know

This exercise works your shoulders and may be done while seated in bed or standing on the floor. Shrug your shoulders as if to indicate you didn't know something. Repeat three times.

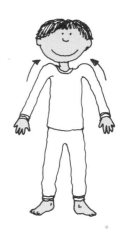

Row, Row, Row Your Boat

This exercise stretches the whole upper body—especially the back and chest. It may be done seated in bed or on the floor. Pretend you are in a boat with oars. Reach out far in front of you and then bring your hands in to your chest with your elbows pointed straight back. If your legs are stretched straight out in front of you and you lean slightly forward, it will also stretch the hamstrings. Repeat three times.

♥ *When your child's eyes are sensitive to light (for instance, when he has a high fever) turn off the lights and use a night-light or a pink bulb instead.*

Airplane

This exercise stretches your sides (obliques) and may be done while seated in bed or standing on the floor. With your arms straight out to your sides, lean to the left and lean to the right. Repeat three times.

♥ *If you make exercising a separate activity, try doing it to music. It's a lot more fun.*

Muscle Man

This exercise works the biceps and may be done seated in bed or standing on the floor. Hold your arms out in front of you or out at the sides, keeping your elbows stationary. Bend your arms at the elbow and make a muscle. You can put a sponge ball in the crook of each elbow and squeeze. Repeat three times.

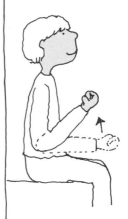

Playing Simple Simon in bed or on the floor is a great way of stretching out stiff or underused muscles. For example, touching the toes, reaching for the ceiling, rolling one shoulder at a time, backward and then forward, are all good exercises.

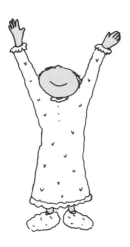

Raise the Bridge and Lower the Bridge

This exercise works the triceps and may be done while seated in bed or on the floor with the knees bent. Put your hands behind your bottom and raise your body up and then lower it, bending your elbows. Repeat three times.

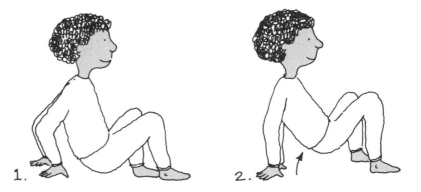

Give Your Teddy a Ride

This exercise works the legs and may be done in bed or on a chair. Sitting at the edge of your bed, place your teddy at your ankles, holding on to his paws. Raise your legs to almost straighten them and then lower your teddy down. Repeat three times.

Steam Shovel

This exercise works your legs and upper body and may be done in bed or on a chair. Sitting at the edge of your bed, place a soccer-size ball between your legs. Lower your legs and raise them, reaching for the ball with your arms. Grab the ball and bring it around your back and place it back between your legs. Repeat three times.

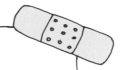

THE SICK-DAY BOX

Annie felt so sorry for her daughter Lisa when she got the chicken pox at age seven that she decided to do everything she could to make Lisa's recovery days memorable. She made a canopy for the bed, brought in lots of balloons, and when Lisa felt a little better, they had their own tea party. But what Lisa remembers more than anything about that terrible week is Annie's invention of the "Sick-Day Box." This is a box that Annie filled with all kinds of surprises and topped with a big sign saying, "My Sick-Day Box." The deal Annie and Lisa made was that the toys and gifts in this box were to be used only when one of the kids was sick. Remembers Lisa, "No matter how much we begged Mom to play with the stuff in my Sick-Day Box on a regular day, she would never let us. At first we were mad, but then it made us feel a lot better to know that when we weren't feeling well the good thing was we got to play with our Sick-Day Box."

Buy and collect the following items, and keep the contents a secret from your child. This box full of suggested surprises is to be used *only* when your child is home sick.

In Jesse Lynch's neighborhood it was customary for friends to lend a favorite toy to the child who was sick for the duration of his illness.

4 new books (see page 109)

4 cassettes (music and/or books on tape) (see page 117)

1 videotape (see page 119)

2 to 4 comic books

2 notebooks (one lined for writing, one unlined for drawing)

Washable markers

A photo album

A disposable camera

Stencils

Puff paints and a T-shirt to decorate

A selection of your child's favorite travel games (see page 82)

Rubber stamps and a stamp pad

Stickers

Puzzles

Wind-up toys

A flipbook

Miniature toys

A deck of cards

2 pairs of dice

A package of Friendly Plastic (available at local craft stores)

White and colored glue

A package of balloons

A set of finger puppets

A miniature stuffed animal

32

Replace your regular light bulbs with colored ones.

Change the aroma in the room by bringing in different mixtures of potpourri. Your child can help you mix them.

DECORATING THE ROOM

The bedroom where a sick child is convalescing doesn't need to be a depressing place. In fact, you can create a new "special" room for his convalescence.

♥

Rya and Jesse Lyons like to take their pillows and blankets and set up camp in the family room instead of staying in their rooms.

Hang a flashlight near the bed. It can comfort your child in the night and is a lot of fun to play with under the covers during the day. (Show him how his skin glows red when he puts his hand over the flashlight in the dark.)

Get out your old baby monitor. Not only can your sick child call you, but he can tell you what he needs and save you some steps. A walkie-talkie works, too.

Have toys and play materials close at hand; use attractive bed covers and let your child wear cheerful, comfortable clothes.

When your child is going to be in bed for more than a day or two, place his bed next to the window. It will bring the outside world into his room.

Make a canopy over your child's bed. Tape a 3-foot dowel (available at the hardware store) to each corner of the bed with masking tape. Cover each dowel with colorful ribbons or streamers by winding them around the stick, as you would in making a Maypole. Using the tape, attach the ribbons or streamers (at least six per dowel) to the ceiling over the center of the bed and extend them to the top of each dowel, to create an instant canopy. Tape the ends of the ribbons to the top of each dowel. For extra flourish, decorate the center of the canopy and the top of each corner with paper flowers. For a special occasion, string miniature white Christmas lights around the room.

Decorate your child's room as if you were decorating for his birthday. Use balloons, crepe paper, and streamers.

A bowl of goldfish placed near the bed can provide hours of amusement.

Position a painting easel by the bed. It can be used for drawing or for display. It's also a perfect place for attaching a Velcro dart board.

Position a mirror so that your child can see into the next room from his bed.

Plastic sandwich bags are ideal for keeping small items, such as crayons, beads, threads, buttons, and dice.

A large hard surface comes in handy for eating, playing games, and doing craft projects. Keep a bed tray handy and place an adjustable ironing board next to the bed. (It's just like a hospital table—when you're finished with it, you can fold it up and put it away!)

Fasten a shoe bag to the wall or to a bulletin board next to the bed (you can use a push pin). Fill the compartments with different useful items—one can hold crayons, another tissues, a third a book, another Band-Aids.

Cover the bed table with a different color cloth every day (plastic works great).

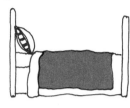

For writing in bed, use a clipboard and tie a pen or a pencil to the top.

Muffin tins and egg cartons are also great for separating small things your child may need.

Hang a string bag filled with different pairs of funny socks next to the bed. Socks on your child's feet make it easier for him each time he has to get out of bed. Having a choice of socks to change into during the day is fun.

A whistle, a bell, or a musical instrument such as a xylophone or a recorder next to the bed gives your patient a way of summoning you. Think of changing the noisemaker of choice each day!

Encourage guests to sign an autograph sheet. Hang an old sheet over the door or tape it to the wall. Provide markers so visitors can leave their doodles, artwork, and well-wishes behind.

Draw and cut out several basic door hanger shapes. Use markers to decorate, draw, and write messages on the hangers. Some ideas to suggest to your patient: Do Not Disturb, No Adults Allowed, On Vacation, Maid Service, Great Brain at Work, Home of the Main Brain, Quiet—Kid at Work, All Dogs Allowed, Only 5 and Under, Knock Three Times and Give the Password.

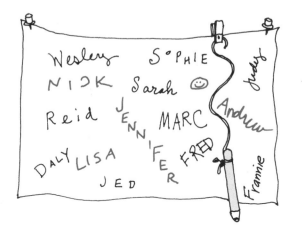

Ice tongs or kitchen tongs tied to the bed with a long string are useful when things have dropped to the floor or are out of reach.

Place a bulletin board near your child's bed. Pin up cards, schedules, funny or attractive pictures, messages, photographs of school friends, and animals from magazines.

You can turn your window shades into maps and murals (this is especially effective and worth the trouble and money for a child who is going to be in bed for an extended period of time). Use white window shades. Draw or paint a new horizon, an abstract design, a sunny garden, a summer dream, a map, a friend. Hang them in the windows (or where you wish there were windows!).

Paint city streets on oilcloth using water-based tempera paints. Let your child use his imagination to create a park, a playground, or a raceway for miniature cars.

Remember the handmade clock your child brought home from kindergarten? If you've discarded it, it's time to make another one. With a large gold brad fastener, attach construction paper hands to the center of a paper plate and write in clock numbers. Whenever a visitor is due, or it's time to take medicine, you can pinpoint the occasion by marking it on the clock.

Hang an oversize calendar by the bed; your child can cross off the days as they pass. Mark when friends are coming to visit, when favorite TV programs are scheduled, or when any special event will be occurring.

A paper shopping bag hung on the bed-post or from a hook will serve as the perfect garbage bag.

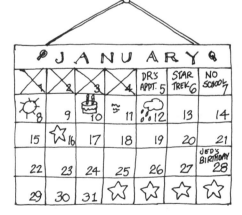

Sometimes a child in bed complains that the covers are too heavy on his legs. Pillows placed along both sides of the legs will hold the covers up.

Projects & Activities

In this section you will find over forty different projects and activities that your child can do when he's home sick. Each project or activity will have one or more symbols next to it. A drawing of a bed means this is a project or an activity that is perfectly fine to do when your child is in bed (it's safe, it's easy, it's not that messy, and it isn't breakable).

A gift-wrapped box means that this project or activity is what we call a "kit": . It includes everything your child will need for that project or activity. You can also put a kit together and bring it to a child who is ill as a gift. We promise it will bring a smile to his face (and to his mom's and dad's!).

Our third symbol is a drawing of one or two happy faces. One face ☺ means this is a project or an activity your child can do alone; two faces ☺☺ means that you need more than one person (and sometimes more than two) to do that activity.

POINT OF VIEW

For a child who is confined to his bed or room, the gift of bringing the outside world in will be most appreciated. Gather together drawing paper, colored pencils, crayons, markers, and Craypas or other pastels. If you can, position your child's bed near the window. A bed tray with an adjustable top can serve as an easel. All your child has to do is look at the world outside and interpret it on paper. Remember—anything goes. A contemporary abstract image is just as wonderful as a perfectly realistic reproduction.

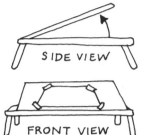

SIDE VIEW

FRONT VIEW

MIRROR IMAGE

Here's a fun drawing challenge. Cut out a photograph from a magazine and then cut the photo in half in either a straight or a zigzag line. Glue one half on a large sheet of white paper or cardboard. Now, using a pencil or a marker, draw the other half. Your child can try to copy the unglued half of the photo or make the "mirror image" any way he sees it.

CUT ON LINE.

LEFT SIDE IS ACTUAL PHOTO.

RIGHT SIDE IS YOUR DRAWING.

40

SWEEPSTAKES

♥

Jeff Buhai remembers entering every contest that he could find. This included ones that came in the mail, ones that were advertised in papers and magazines, and ones that were advertised on television. "I never won anything," says Jeff, "but the point was to fill up the time with the excitement of the possibility of winning every time I filled out one of those forms."

WHAT'S WRONG?

With a collection of old catalogs and magazines, a child can have a great deal of fun creating a "What's Wrong with This Picture?" collage. Look through some magazines and find a large detailed photo or illustration, then glue it onto a sheet of construction paper. From another picture cut out items similar to ones that appear in the first, such as faces, bodies, arms, legs, and glue those onto the first picture in the appropriate spots. For example, a carnival scene might have the people's faces replaced with animal faces, or a photograph of a school yard might have the children's heads or bodies replaced with those of adults. The possibilities for creating whimsical and silly new pictures are limitless.

CARBON COPY

Here's a trick that gives your child two drawings for the effort of one (well, almost!). Take lots of different color crayons and fill in one whole side of a piece of white or light-colored paper (Marc Gilbar and his friend Jon Kasdan's tip from trying this at school is that dark crayons work better than light ones). When you're done coloring, put the finished paper face down on top of a blank sheet of paper. Now draw a picture or write a message with a ballpoint pen, pressing down hard, on the clean side of the crayoned sheet. Whatever you draw will transfer itself to the bottom sheet in a multicolored design.

1. COVER PAPER WITH CRAYONS IN DIFFERENT COLORS.

2. TURN CRAYONED SHEET OVER ON TOP OF CLEAN PAPER.

3. DRAW ON BACK OF CRAYONED SHEET WITH A BALLPOINT PEN.

4. REMOVE TOP SHEET AND YOU HAVE A MULTICOLORED LINE.

41

"DECORATE-YOUR-CAST" KIT

Here are some ideas to brighten up that cast:

★ Decorate it with quick-drying puff paints or colored glue. Sarah Israel covered her cast with puff paints that had glue in them and stuck sequins and plastic jewels right in the paint. Elmer's makes colored glues that are particularly effective.

★ Collect a variety of permanent marking pens in different colors for autographs.

★ Use stencils of funny images. Just color them in with markers.

★ Marc Gilbar's friend Jeremy Konner has had occasion to wear casts on various parts of his body. The latest cast was fluorescent green. To preserve the integrity of the fluorescent theme, Jeremy carried around pens in various fluorescent colors for his friends to sign their names.

★ Rubber stamps can make very funny decorations—especially those that say, "Property of. . ." or "This belongs to. . ." or "Award-winning. . . ."

★ Somehow people always think of cast decorating as permanent, but with a variety of stickers, your child can change his decorations daily. He can choose a theme for a day and the next day change his mind.

★ If your child is wearing a cast around a holiday (for instance, Christmas or the Fourth of July), consider decorating the cast in the theme of that holiday using appropriate colors, items, and pictures.

♥

Jed Schwartz, Wesley's dad, said that when Wesley broke his leg, a garbage bag and duct tape worked fine for keeping his leg dry when showering.

♥

With masking tape, fasten a large sheet of wrapping paper to the wall face down and have your child use it as a drawing board. Our friend Joyce Bogart Trabulus went a step further. When her son Evan broke his arm, she bought a metal roller, fastened it to the wall next to his bed, and put a roll of butcher paper on it. Whenever Evan completed a picture or a message, he would tear it off, pull down some more paper, and be ready for the next time.

Cookie cutters are useful to small children for tracing and coloring, but they can also be used by children of any age in making greeting cards.

STENCILING

There has been a resurgence in the popularity of this time-honored craft. Many toy stores and craft stores carry bags of stencils. They are great to use to create drawings and to make calendars, cards, and the like. For example, take stencils of letters, spell your child's name with the stencils, arrange them so they're askew, and color them in with crayons. To make a more elaborate design, take a stencil of a favorite image (like Superman or a train or a car) and superimpose that somewhere over the letters. Color this in with markers to create a variety of textures. You can keep on going with this—superimposing stencil over stencil with crayons, markers, or pencils until you end up with a multi-layered painting.

COLLAGE

"Collage," often called "found art," is a perfect project for a child who is stuck at home. First, choose an idea, a theme, a color (or, you may just decide that your collage will include everything but the kitchen sink), then collect items that somehow relate to your idea. You can draw your own pictures, use stencils, or cut them out of magazines or newspapers (fashion magazines and comics are all good sources), or you can use old toys, cutout letters, fabric, sheet music, buttons, small kitchen items. Arrange the materials that you've chosen on a large piece of foam board or stiff cardboard. When you're sure you've got a design you like, glue them in place with white glue or with a hot glue gun. When it's dry, you're done. For a variation, spray paint the entire collage in one color.

MAP WORLD

Children are fascinated by maps of the world. Using maps in art projects is both a way of teaching them about geography and a way of showing them how easy it is to alter the world (great for kids who want to feel more in control of their environment). You can buy an inexpensive paperback atlas in many bookstores.

Choose any map from the atlas, tear it out, and follow our suggestions below to make your own "Map World." For example, if you use a map of the United States you can:

★ Color in all the mountains, shade in the rivers and other bodies of water, and put a star sticker on the capital of each state.

★ Cut out each state and make a collage of your new United States. You can make an abstract design, you can group all the large states on one side and all the small ones on another, or you can switch states that your child has an interest in (if you live in Kansas City and Grandma lives in New York and your child would like her to be closer to you, just move New York next to Kansas).

★ Arrange the states into a new alphabetized United States. Start with Alabama in the northwest corner and move down and around until you end up with Wyoming where Florida used to be.

When you're done with the maps in the atlas, you might try drawing a map of your own neighborhood. Using graph paper or plain white paper, draw in the streets, the houses, the parks, and whatever monuments or landmarks your child loves.

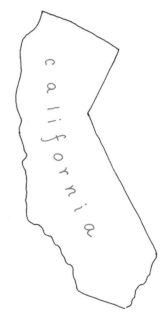

44

ANIMATION WHEEL

Here is a way of making a "phenakistoscope," the first animation device. (It was invented in the 1830s and was the forerunner of the motion picture.)

Cut an 8½-inch-round circle out of white construction paper. With a pencil, divide it into twelve equal segments. Cut out a slot, 1 inch long by ⅜ inch wide, at the end of each radius (see drawing).

On a piece of white paper, draw (with a template or a compass) twelve 1½-inch-round circles. Number the circles 1 through 12, then draw an image in sequence in each circle. Be sure to plan the story so the character or object will move (it can be a changing abstract shape, a bouncing ball, a running figure). The key is to show change over the course of the twelve different frames.

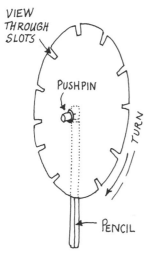

VIEW THROUGH SLOTS

PUSHPIN

TURN

PENCIL

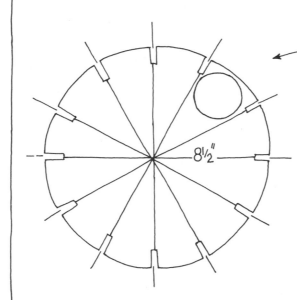

8½"

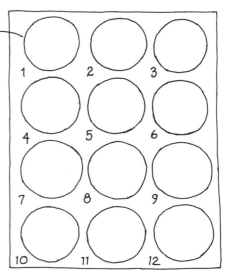

SPIN

When the drawings are done, cut out the circles, keeping them in numerical order. Glue the cutout circles in sequence around the edge of the larger circle, placing them between the radius lines (see drawing).

Stick a pushpin through the center of the circle into the eraser head of a pencil placed under the cartoon wheel. Make sure that the wheel will spin easily on the pin. Place a mirror in front of your child as he holds the cartoon wheel in his hand, cartoon images toward the mirror. Have him hold the pencil in one hand, and use the other hand to spin the wheel. He should look at the cartoon with his eye close to the slots as they spin.

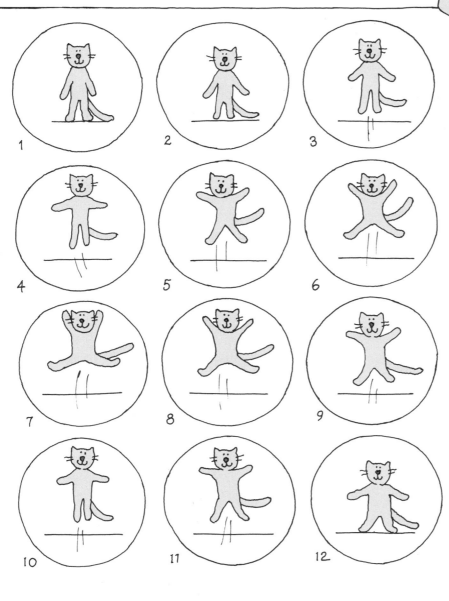

1   2   3

4   5   6

7   8   9

10   11   12

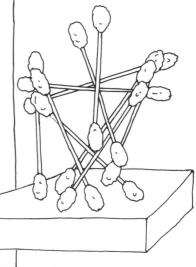

♥ When Jill's brother Andrew was small he had to go through a series of tests at Children's Hospital in New York. He remembers how a special present went a long way in making a good memory out of a potentially bad one. He still arranges a treat for himself when an unpleasant doctor's visit is scheduled.

Q-TIP QUEST

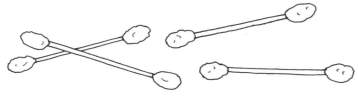

Here's how you can make a Q-tip sculpture: Get a large piece of foam board or stiff cardboard and some white or colored glue. Dip each end of each Q-tip into the glue and then place it on your surface to form a base. As the glue sets, add more Q-tips. The end result is an abstract sculpture that can then be spray painted in one or more colors.

BLOTTERS

You can get a large blotter at any art or stationery store. The beauty of "blotters" is that you can never make the same design twice. Adults may remember blotters as being messy because the inks that were used always ended up on our fingers. Today, you can use felt-tip pens, which will make wonderful abstract designs. Look for blotters that have a backing so the ink will not leak through.

DRAWING ON A MIRROR

When your child is in bed for a long time, having a mirror nearby may cheer him up (unless he has the chicken pox, in which case take down all the mirrors!). Using puff paints and permanent markers, decorate around the edges of a large unbreakable mirror. You can even glue things to the mirror like large beads, plastic jewels, old toy cars, and other collage materials. The object is to create a pretty, cheerful, even funny, design, so that whenever your child looks in the mirror it will make him smile.

COMIC MIX-UP

For a child like Marc Gilbar, who loves comics, the thought of being stuck in bed with his entire comic book collection is nothing less than heaven. Marc takes it a step further—he collects comics from newspapers, takes his favorite strips, cuts them into sections, and mixes them up to create new strips.

"MAKE-A-CARTOON" MOVIE

In the *Penny Whistle Birthday Party Book*, the children at the Superheroes Party made a cartoon film of a face with changing expressions. Marc Gilbar, our own cartoon expert, suggested that this would be a fun way to cheer up a sick child. Get a three-ring binder, which will be the "animation board." Tape the binder to a flat work surface that can be used in bed, making sure that the binder cannot move. Have on hand at least thirty sheets of unlined three-holed paper. Using a thick black marker, draw simple figures in sequence, one per page, each slightly different from the last one. After one drawing is completed, place it in the binder and top it with a blank sheet. Now draw your next figure on this blank sheet. Make sure that the next figure is drawn right on top of the previous one. (You will be putting the sheets in backward, with the first sheet of the cartoon at the bottom of the pile.) It will take between twenty and thirty sheets to complete the animated cartoon. Be sure to include a title sheet and place it under all the rest.

Place a video camera in a fixed position on a tripod and focus it toward the animation board. Shoot the "title board" of the cartoon first, holding the image for about ten seconds. Then film each sheet for one second (basically you turn the camera on, then off). That's it—when you play the videotape back, you will have a full-fledged cartoon!

❤
Another type of clay that is good to use is Fimo, available at craft stores. It comes in a variety of colors as well as types that glow in the dark.

BAKER'S CLAY

4 cups unsifted all-purpose flour
1 cup salt
1½ cups cold water

Preheat the oven to 350°F.
Stir together the flour, salt, and water until everything is well blended. Turn the dough out onto a lightly floured board and knead vigorously for about 5 minutes until a smooth, pliable dough is formed. Add some more flour to the board if necessary to prevent sticking in the early stages of kneading. The finished dough should not be sticky.

Note: Store the dough in a plastic bag to prevent it from drying out. Bake your creations for 50 to 60 minutes or until they feel solid and are ivory to light brown in color. Cool. Decorate or paint with acrylic paints and spray with shellac. The dough should be baked within 4 to 5 hours of making it.

CLAY

For young children, playing with clay is heavenly. The tactile feeling of mushy clay in their hands is always a hit. For projects you'd like to keep, we recommend using clay like Sculpey or making your own baker's clay, which can be molded, baked, and painted as you'd like. Young children (ages three to six), whose fine-hand coordination and ability to create "realistic" forms is still developing, should be encouraged to use cookie cutters. Remember that cookie cutter shapes can be turned into pendants (just punch a hole before you bake), bookends (add a flat piece of clay to the bottom of each cutout so that it will stand up straight), or paperweights.

Children aged seven to ten might enjoy using clay to make dollhouses, different animals (snakes, worms, bugs), or Lisa Gilbar's favorite, food. A clay box can be made by forming six straight and even sides and using a ball of clay for the handle. Or how about a tea set? Saucers are easy, cups can be shaped with your fingers, and a teapot can be made by forming the clay into the right shape and adding a spout and a handle. To make any of these shapes, roll out the clay until it is about a ¼ inch thick. Then with a cookie cutter or a dull butter knife, cut out whatever shapes you need.

Older children, or those with good fine-hand coordination, can make jewelry (this will keep your sick child busy for hours, since jewelry making is often addictive!). Start with beads made from Sculpture Clay by Sculpey. A package of ten bricks of clay, in ten colors, will make about two hundred beads (each brick makes about twenty beads). Break off pieces of clay the size of marbles and roll them, one at a time, between your hands to form beads. Try combining two colors of clay in one bead. Poke a hole through each bead with a toothpick.

When you're finished forming your beads, place them on a cookie sheet and bake at 350°F for twenty minutes; the beads should not touch while baking. When done, remove them from the oven and let them cool (they will continue to harden as they cool). You can leave each bead plain or paint a design using acrylic tempera paint or draw patterns with permanent markers. To make necklaces, bracelets, or earrings, just string the beads on elastic thread or hang from earring hooks.

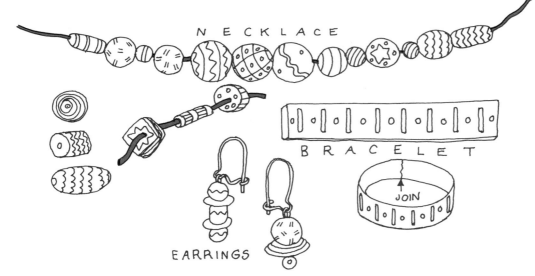

NECKLACE

BRACELET

JOIN

EARRINGS

FANTASY SCULPTURE

"Fantasy sculpture" is your child's vision of whatever he wants to make. Like collage, it's an easy and absorbing project made of bits and pieces found around the house. Collect all kinds of items that have interesting shapes that can be painted. Consider using miniature toys, blocks, ice-cream sticks, old board game pieces, playing cards, bottle caps, buttons, thimbles, paper cups, forks, spoons—anything goes. Arrange these on a sturdy base of foam board or stiff cardboard and then glue them on any way you want. Remember that the sculpture doesn't have to be flat; you can glue things one on top of the other for added dimension. When you're done you can leave it as is or spray paint it in one or more colors.

QUICK JEWELRY

Annie's sister, Dr. Sonia Israel, and her daughter Sarah discovered Friendly Plastic a couple of years ago at their local craft store and have been making jewelry with it ever since. We used their instructions for pins as Hanukkah gifts in *The Penny Whistle Christmas Party Book*. When Sarah broke her arm last year, she made the happy discovery that Friendly Plastic was easy enough to mold into pins and earrings with just one hand!

All you need is a bag of Friendly Plastic and a bowl of warm water. Just dip the plastic pieces in the water, one at a time, and then mold them with your hand(s) into any interesting shape. To make earrings, the pieces can be pierced and hung on earring hooks or you can make a brooch by gluing a pin to the back of each one.

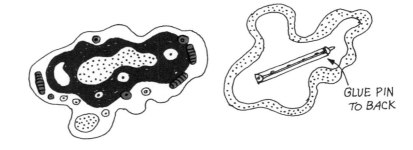

GLUE PIN TO BACK

ROLLED PAPER BEADS

Susan Russell taught her daughters Cory and Megan how to make paper beads when they were very young. This is a project children aged four to seven will need help with; older kids will have no trouble doing it themselves. First, cut triangle shapes from pieces of paper (newspaper or comic book paper will do well, but the magazine paper, which is slick and colorful, works best). The size of the triangle will determine the size of the bead that is formed; small triangles make smaller beads. Starting with the wide end, roll the paper triangle tightly over a pencil or a pen. When the roll of paper is finished, rub a bit of glue under the pointed end; hold firmly for a couple of seconds while the glue sets, then slide your bead off the pencil. To make bracelets or necklaces, you can string the beads on colored yarn and tie the ends together.

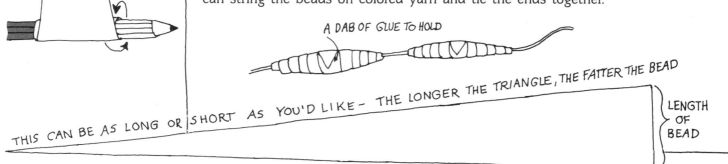

A DAB OF GLUE TO HOLD

THIS CAN BE AS LONG OR SHORT AS YOU'D LIKE— THE LONGER THE TRIANGLE, THE FATTER THE BEAD

LENGTH OF BEAD

THE PERFECT POP-UP GET-WELL CARD

Your child can send the "Perfect Pop-Up Get-Well Card" to a friend. Fold a piece of heavy paper (8½ by 5½ inches) in half. This will be the card. Cut a strip of paper (6½ by 3 inches). Make a mark at the following measurements on the strip, from left to right: 1½ inches, 3 inches, 1 inch, and 1 inch. From each mark, draw a light vertical line on your strip. Make sure that the third and fourth sections are the same size.

Draw and color a bed or any other get-well scene on the first three sections of the strip of paper. The fourth section will be a blank tab. (A tab is a section of paper that will be attached to another piece of paper. You do not draw on the tab.) Make the folds indicated on the illustration. Remember, a mountain fold is upward like a mountain. A valley fold is downward like a valley.

Apply glue to the front side of the tab. Fold the tab back and place it on the bottom section of the card, with the edge of the tab on the fold line of the card.

Apply glue to the blank side of the top section of the strip and close the card. Press down firmly. Wait for the glue to dry. Open the card carefully. The top section should now be glued in place. The scene will pop up when the card is opened and collapse when the card is closed.

Decorate the front and inside of the card.

♥
When Sydny Miner was a teenager she had surgery and couldn't wash her own hair. Until she got well, her mother treated her to regular visits to the beauty parlor to be shampooed.

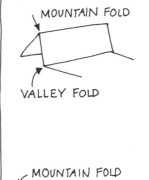

MOUNTAIN FOLD

VALLEY FOLD

VALLEY FOLD

MOUNTAIN FOLD

MOUNTAIN FOLD

3. MAKE FOLDS.

4¼" 5½"

1. FOLD 11-BY-8½-INCH PAPER IN HALF.

| 1 | 2 | 3 | 4 |

←1½"→ ←3"→ ←1"→ ←1"→ 3"

2. MARK OFF 4 SECTIONS ON A PIECE OF 6½-BY-3-INCH PAPER.

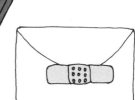

7. CLOSE THE ENVELOPE WITH A BAND-AID.

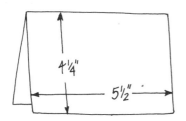

1
2
3
4
TAB

4. DRAW BED AND COLOR.

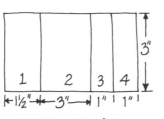

5. DECORATE THE INSIDE OF THE CARD.

GLUE TOP SECTION IN PLACE

GLUE

TAB SIDE FOLDED UNDER AND GLUED

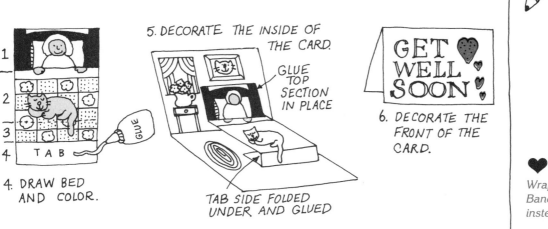

GET WELL SOON

6. DECORATE THE FRONT OF THE CARD.

♥
Wrap your get-well gifts with Band-Aids and use gauze instead of ribbons.

ETCH 'N' SKETCH

Your child may be familiar with this project because it is a favorite at many preschools. Take a piece of white paper and color it in completely using crayons of different colors. When you're done, take a thick black crayon and color over the entire drawing. Now, using a metal screw or nail (or for younger children, a metal nail file), scratch out your design. Everywhere you scratch, the black will come off and the colors will show through. When you are done you can take a paper towel and gently rub the surface of your picture. This will give the finished product a polished look. (If your child does this project in bed, be sure to put something over the blankets and sheets, as the crayon scrapings can make a mess of the sheets!)

♥

Vinyl tablecloths are great to put over the child's bed when he is working on projects. They protect the blankets and sheets and are easy to wipe clean.

POLISH
DRAWING WHEN
ALL FINISHED

ROSE-COLORED GLASSES

Make a pair of "rose-colored glasses" for your child to wear in bed. It will give him a new look at things in his room and the people around him. The glasses are so easy to make, you may want to create more than one pair, each with different color lenses. You will need some red or pink cellophane and some old glasses frames with the lenses removed. (You can also cut out "glasses" from cardboard.) Cut the cellophane to fit the eye holes and cover them. Tape the cellophane in place. For a more intense effect, add another layer of cellophane.

ADD
PIPE
CLEANER

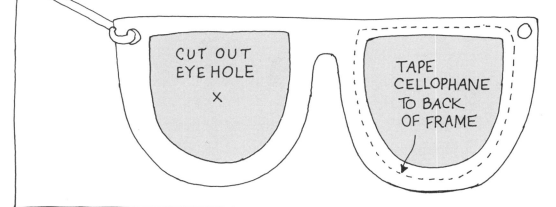

CUT OUT
EYE HOLE
X

TAPE
CELLOPHANE
TO BACK
OF FRAME

MAGIC MOMENTS

A child who is homebound for an extended period is likely to have some visitors. If he's up for a little humor, why not surprise or maybe even shock them! Marc's cousin Sky Gilbar hated the time he had to stay in bed with strep throat. To cheer him up, he and his mom, Inge, made animals that hid quietly in Sky's bed until his grandparents, Sylvia and Marty, came by to visit.

Sky had a bed snake that actually slithered in and around the bed. Here's how to make one of your own: Take a strip of satin and cut it into the shape of a 5-foot-long, 10-inch-wide snake. With a black permanent marker, draw eyes at one end. Now pull a 5-foot-long piece of thread through the head of the snake and tie a knot. Take the other end of the thread and loop it around your child's wrist. Let the snake "sleep" quietly at the end of the bed under the covers. As visitors come around the bed, instruct your child to lie very still as if he were sleeping and then suddenly move his wrist to make the "snake" slither over the covers and up his arm or against his visitors. The reactions will be worth recording, so you might want to have a camera on hand for an action shot.

Here's another old Halloween trick: Stuff a long pair of socks until they are very full (you can use cotton, pieces of fabric, or hand towels). Put large shoes on the feet and place them so they are peeking out of the blanket at the foot of the bed. Or how about scaring guests with an extra arm that could appear from behind your child? Take an old sweater and cut off the sleeves. Stuff them with socks. Sky once tied a rubber glove filled with cotton balls to the end of the arm!

❤ *Do you have somewhere else your child can lie down? A daybed or chaise longue, perhaps, to let the patient be with the family.*

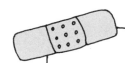
CUTOUT PAPER CIRCUS

To make this paper circus you will need scissors, white construction paper or oak tag, markers or crayons, string, glue, and a stapler.

Below are instructions for an elephant, lion, clown, ringmaster, and a seal balancing a ball. The pair of trapeze artists can be made by using the clown pattern adding an inch for the outstretched arms. Glue them together and attach to the swing. The swing is a bar cut from paper and hung with string. The girl riding the elephant is cut from a smaller rectangle and notched on the bottom to fit over the elephant's back.

Using the patterns below you can expand this one-ring circus into a full-blown three-ring circus adding all kinds of events. These patterns can be Xeroxed and enlarged. We suggest using them as a guide and drawing your own designs.

LION HEAD

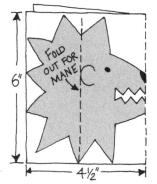

6"

4½"

1. TAKE 6-BY-9-INCH PAPER AND FOLD IN HALF.

2. DRAW HEAD PLACING NOSE ON FOLD.

3. CUT OUT AND TURN OVER.

4. DRAW DETAILS ON THE OTHER SIDE.

ELEPHANT HEAD

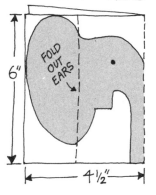

6"

4½"

FOLD OUT EARS

LION & ELEPHANT BODY

6" X 9"

1. DRAW BODY ON FOLDED SHEET PLACING THE TOP OF BACK ON FOLD.

2. CUT OUT AND DRAW DETAILS ON THE OTHER SIDE.

GLUE TAIL

TAIL: CUT 1

ADD TAIL

GLUE ON TUSKS

CUT 1 TAIL

CUT 2 TUSKS

B

A

B A

1. TO ASSEMBLE HEAD TO BODY STAPLE RIGHT SIDE (A) TO (A).

2. FAN OUT THE ELEPHANT'S EARS AND THE LION'S MANE.

GLUE STRING

GLUE A TOOTHPICK

CUT OUT

CUT OUT

FOLD ARM

CUT OUT

CUT OUT

6"

4"

FOLD FOR TABS

1. DRAW FIGURES ON A 4-BY-6-INCH SHEET OF PAPER.

2. CUT OUT.

3. FOLD DOWN CENTER TO HELP THE FIGURE STAND.

FOLD FRONT

FOLD BACK

CUT OUT

CUT OUT

6" SQUARE

CUT 2

CUT SLIT

CUT OUT

SEAL

1. FOLD 6-INCH SQUARE SHEET OF PAPER ON THE DIAGONAL.
2. DRAW SEAL.
3. CUT OUT AND DRAW SEAL ON OTHER SIDE.
4. GLUE THE BALL TO THE NOSE.
5. FOLD IN TABS FOR STAND.

STRING

PAPER BAR

GLUE TO BAR

7"

GLUE

7"

When you have completed your circus you can make the ring by stapling three strips of paper (1 by 11 inches) to form a circle. For the grand finale make a sign announcing "The Greatest Show on Earth."

THE GREATEST SHOW ON EARTH

56

♥

When Remy Weber's nursery school teacher left to have her baby, the class and parents made a quilt as a gift. They cut out simple squares of muslin and each child drew a picture of himself on the square using fabric crayons. One of the mothers sewed it into a quilt. This is a great gift for someone who is sick or for a sick child to work on with a parent.

FOREVER FELT

Younger children love playing with felt shapes and a felt board. Felt is the perfect material for the sick child in bed to work with, since it's soft, it can't break or tear, it's clean, and it won't fall off the board. Nursery-age kids will be happy to make designs from different shapes and colors. You can also create a matching game (cut out duplicate shapes, lay out one set, and have your child match them), play tic-tac-toe, cut out shapes of letters and numbers, or cut out shapes of people (heads, bodies, legs, arms) and then face parts (mouths, both smiling and frowning, eyes and eyebrows, ears, noses) so you can add expressions.

To make this felt kit, either for "The Sick-Day Box" (see page 31) or as a present for a sick child, here's what you'll need: a cardboard box at least 12 inches square, squares of felt in assorted colors (fabric stores carry felt already cut into 12-inch squares), and white glue. Glue one piece of felt to the bottom of the box. Cut the other squares into shapes, or leave them whole and include a pair of scissors if the child is going to do the cutting. Place the felt pieces (and scissors) in the box, and that's it!

SPONGIES

When the doctor says it's okay for your recovering child to have a bath, make it a special treat by adding sponge animals to his bath water. You can buy sponges in a variety of shapes in any toy store or drugstore, but it's also fun to cut out these shapes for yourself. Just cut sponges of different colors and sizes into animal or abstract "monster" shapes. Once they are cut, you can outline the edges with permanent markers and add detail to the faces. You can also cut out simple shapes like flowers, houses, dolls, and so on. When the markers have dried, just wet the sponge, press it on the tile wall of the bath, and press the water out—it will stick!

PAPER DOLLS

Jill Weber's favorite activity whenever she was sick was to cut out "paper dolls." She began by collecting "Betsy McCall" paper dolls from *McCalls* magazine. However, she soon tired of them so she started designing her own paper dolls and clothes. Below you will see our infamous Penny Cat with his very own wardrobe. Xerox the drawings, color them, then cut them out. Paste Penny Cat on cardboard so he is stiff. Try designing your own paper dolls and clothes.

Barbara Schwartz's favorite memory is of her father cutting out paper dolls with her whenever she was sick.

MONTH CALENDAR

For the child who will be home for more than a week, making his own calendar might have special appeal. The materials you will need are simple: foam board or cardboard (approximately 24 by 18 inches), scissors, markers or crayons, white glue, and pictures from magazines.

On a piece of foam board, mark off boxes for the number of days in the month. Make each box about 2 inches square so you have enough room to write. Mark the days of the week across the top and the number of each day in the appropriate box. From magazines, cut out small pictures depicting special days of the month, such as holidays or birthdays of famous people.

As each day begins, have your child write in the plans for that day. During the day he can add things that happen to him that he thinks are important. In that way, the calendar will remain as a kind of diary when he has recovered.

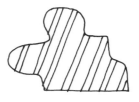

♥ *Compoz-A-Puzzle, made by Rubber Stamps of America (Saxton River, Vermont), contains four blank twenty-eight-piece puzzles with four envelopes. Your child assembles the puzzles and makes his own designs using pens, pencils, rubber stamps, markers, or paints. They can be disassembled and stored in the envelopes provided—or mailed to friends.*

PUZZLES

If your child is a jigsaw puzzle freak ("puzzle fans are always called 'puzzle freaks,'" says Gabe Gordon, age fourteen. He should know, since he's been collecting and solving them since he was five!), remember to stock up on a variety when your child is going to be home for a while. You can also make your own by pasting colorful magazine pictures onto large pieces of cardboard and cutting them into random pieces.

Any kind of puzzle is great to store at home for those times when your child is sick.

SEWING CARDS

Sewing can be a satisfying activity, one that doesn't take much energy yet results in immediate gratification for young children. Stitching a large picture frame is probably enough of a challenge for a young child, while older children might fill in objects and details using several colors and different weights of yarn.

You will need stiff colored cardboard, several long strands of colored yarn, a large needlepoint needle, and a hand-held hole punch.

Cut the cardboard into any shape you like (young kids may want to trace shapes using cookie cutters). You will probably want to punch the cards, thread the needle, and knot the end of the yarn for your preschooler; kids over five can do this themselves. (Use a large sewing needle with a very rounded tip.) Have your child stitch the yarn from hole to hole all the way around the outline. Tie the yarn to finish or have him sew back in the opposite direction to fill in all the spaces. Older children can punch holes in the center to form a more detailed design, and then fill it in with a variety of colors.

FUNNY BALLOON PEOPLE

This is an easy and fun activity for children of all ages! Buy a package of balloons in assorted colors. Blow up one balloon and knot the end. For young children, simply draw faces on the balloons (front and back) with markers and hang them around the room. Older kids can draw a pattern to create feet with or without shoes (see drawing). Trace the pattern onto tissue paper, draw the foot shape on foam board, then cut the foot shape out. Cut slits as shown. Decorate the feet with markers. You can even punch out holes for yarn "shoelaces." Now insert the knotted end of the balloon into the feet, so the balloon person will stand up. Decorate the balloon with markers to create facial features, eyeglasses, or whatever. You can add jewelry, a stretch headband, and yarn for hair.

Each of these balloons becomes another friend to keep your child company. This is a good activity for your child to share with a visiting friend.

← SLIT

SLIDE IN BALLOON KNOT

BED BEANBAGS

We learned this trick from our friend and collaborator, Beth Yow, who broke her arm in the fourth grade. Beth's mom, Sally, was a beanbag expert, having made many of them for both Beth and her sister, Laura. Since Beth had only one arm to work with that time, Sally took the beanbags she'd made and sewed a six-foot length of elastic to each. Beth had a brass bed, so it was easy for Sally to tie one end of the elastic to one of the brass bars (if your child doesn't have a brass or four-poster bed, you can tie one end to a drawer handle or a door handle within easy reach of the bed). To set up the game, cut out four circles from four different color pieces of paper. The circles should be 7 inches, 6 inches, 5 inches, and 3 inches in diameter. With a thick black marker, write a different score on each circle (for example, 25, 50, 75, and 100), with the 100 being the smallest circle and the 25 being the largest circle. Tape the circles to the wall across from the bed (you can also use a wall to either side of the bed as long as it's not too close).

To play, your child throws the beanbags at the targets, adding up his score as he goes along. Each time he throws, the beanbags will bounce back (or he can pull them back) to him, so he will never have to get out of bed.

SEW 6 FEET OF ELASTIC

6 FEET

3"

5"

6"

7"

MINI DIORAMA

Dioramas rank high as favorite school projects for many kids including all three Brokaw girls. Since the girls loved these miniature scenes, Meredith tried to keep on hand the materials necessary for constructing a diorama for those days when someone was "under the weather." Here are the materials needed for a jungle scene: a shoe box, white glue or a glue gun, a picture of woods cut out from a magazine or a wall calendar, an assortment of natural materials (nuts, leaves, tree branches, rocks, sand, stones, twigs, dried flowers, weeds, available in your backyard, craft stores, and florists), clay, and as a final touch—a miniature clip-on monkey.

First, glue the woods scene to the inside bottom of the box. Now stand the shoe box up so the background is upright, then arrange and glue all the accessories for the woods on your "forest floor." Press the lump of clay into the sand and stick a branch or some twigs into it. Finally, clip the little monkey to the branch.

♥ *To make a sports diorama, cut out the appropriate sports figures from sports magazines, paste them on light cardboard, and glue them standing upright or against the back of the shoe box. You can cut out lots of faces and glue them on the back of the box so they'll look like the crowd in the bleachers.*

♥ *When Jason Bloom injured his shoulder skiing, he tied the elastic to his good arm, threw the beanbag at the target, and pulled it back to him.*

♥ *Have your child decorate a T-shirt and wear it in bed.*

RINGTOSS BOX

This is a great game for your child to play right from his bed. You can buy various ringtoss games at toy stores or you can make your own. You'll need a strong cardboard box with a lid, scissors or an X-acto knife, ten wooden clothespins, a marker, and three to five rubber jar rings.

Cut two rows of five evenly spaced holes in the lid of the box with scissors or an X-acto knife. (Be sure that the holes are smaller in diameter than the clothespins so the fit will be snug and the clothespins will stand straight up.) Insert the clothespins into the holes so that they are sticking out of the top of the lid, and close the lid. Number the holes from 1 to 10. Place the box at the foot of the bed. Have your child toss the jar rings over the clothespins and add up his score.

MINI MASKS

With a supply of Halloween half masks on hand, your child and his visitors can cheer up the day. These masks are available all year round, but if you want to make your own, here's how: Take a square piece of paper about 3 inches on each side. Draw eyes along the top edge and a big mouth near the bottom; for a nose, draw a circle that is about the size of a nickel. Cut out enough of the center area of the circle so that you can fit this mini mask securely on your nose.

Now decorate the mask (homemade or store-bought) with puff paints, sequins, feathers, glitter, or anything else you desire. Encourage your child to wear his mask at different times. You can also make masks to fit different moods and have your child wear the one that fits his particular mood at various times during the day.

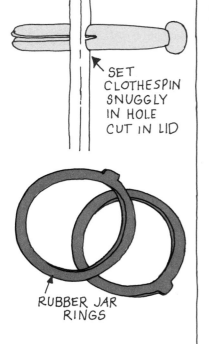

SET CLOTHESPIN SNUGGLY IN HOLE CUT IN LID

RUBBER JAR RINGS

Plastic men or animals attached to homemade parachutes (men's hankies) are great fun when thrown off a bed.

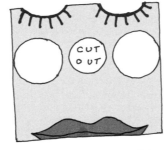

CANDY HOUSE

Making a "candy house" is one of our favorite activities. It's hard to count all of the structures that we've made over the years, but since they're so easy to do, consider constructing one as a "feeling better" activity with your child.

Take a small box—say a milk carton or shoe box—and cover it with Royal Icing. Decorate it by pressing different kinds of candy into the icing. When done you can put it up for display, but advise your child to resist the temptation to eat it (unless your doctor says it's okay) lest he end up sick again!

♥
ROYAL ICING

1 cup sifted confectioner's sugar
1 large egg white
Food coloring

Mix the powdered sugar and egg white. You may tint the icing with a few drops of food coloring. (Fewer drops make a lighter frosting; more drops make it darker.)

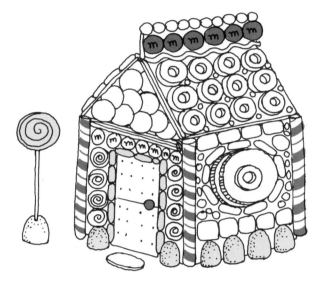

TENT CITY

Lisa Gilbar's best memory of when she was sick as a child is that she got to make her famous "tents." From morning to night, Lisa could be found stretching sheets over chairs, beds, bookcases, tables, all to create large tents. Then, with her sleeping bag and pillow in tow, she would move into the tent—that's where her food would be served, where her reading would be done, and where her friends would be invited to visit. And somehow, even taking medicine wasn't quite so onerous when it was given in the tent.

♥

When Andrew Schwartz had scarlet fever as a small child, he set up camp in his mom's bed every day until he was well. Each day she would come upstairs and find her bed transformed into the theme of the day—a castle, a freeway with Matchbox cars, or a battlefield with little GI Joes deep in combat.

BE SURE TO KEEP FABRIC AWAY FROM THE BULB.

VISITORS' SKETCHBOOK

Keep a spiral notebook or a sketchbook and pens by your child's bedside. Make sure that every visitor that enters the room, no matter how many times he goes in or out, writes a personal message, signs a funny autograph (fibbing is encouraged—sign in as any celebrity you like), or draws a special picture.

MAKING A SKETCHBOOK

For any child who likes to draw, giving him a sketchbook of his own is a great idea. Provide your child with a collection of pencils, crayons, and markers in a broad range of colors and watch even the most timid and ill child be inspired to create. Best of all, such a sketchbook will be something he can look back at when he's older.

REBUS WRITING

For a twist on writing, create a sentence made up not only of words and syllables but of pictures, mathematical symbols, numbers, and letters as well. Write down your favorite story or create a new one, then rewrite it in "rebus writing." Use pictures and symbols cut from magazines or drawn by hand.

For example, "The bear and I ate a peanut butter sandwich" would look like this:

A BOOK ABOUT ME

Delia Ephron recently wrote a wonderful book called *This Is My Life* (Running Dog Press), which would make a precious gift for a sick eight- or nine-year-old child. Your child can also make his own version. Just supply him with a notebook and a pen and have him put together a book about his own life. Gather mementos such as photographs, drawings, ticket stubs, miniature souvenirs, a favorite cartoon, get-well cards, and letters—anything that can be pasted into a book. This gives the child who must be in bed on a longer basis a particularly good way of expressing his feelings about his experiences.

LET IT ALL HANG OUT

This is an invention that your child will love even when he's feeling better. Hang a clothesline across your child's room (you can fasten it by tying it to the bedposts or stapling it to the wall using an electric stapler, or you can use one of those clotheslines that have suction cups attached to the ends) and you will have an instant art gallery to display your child's artwork (use wooden clothespins to hang the pictures). Your child can use the line to hang stories he has written, spell words in big letters, or display his collection of get-well cards.

Ryan Donnelly is six years old and has brittle bones disease, which means he is small for his age and his bones break easily. When he was two, he began to wonder why he was different from other children. His mom tried to find a book to help him understand, but she couldn't find one—so they made a book together. They took pictures of things Ryan liked to do and of things his mom, dad, and doctor did to take care of him, and then they decided what to write under each picture. Ryan takes his "Special Boy Book" to school with him and lets the other kids read it—when he's not giving them rides on his red electric wheelchair!

A tip from Sybil Goldrich: Start an art exhibit in your child's room. Hang everything he creates until he gets better.

HEADLINE

1 COLUMN

Today is

|← 3¼" →|

TYPE OR
WRITE IN A
COLUMN AND
THEN PASTE
ON PAGE —

ADD IN
DRAWINGS
AND PICTURES.

PUBLISHING A NEWSPAPER

If the creative juices start bubbling over in your homebound child, suggest that he put together a newspaper or a newsletter. That will provide a focus that will keep him busy for at least an afternoon! When Marc was twelve, his sixth-grade teacher, Jill Schiff, gathered a group of children after school to make their own newspapers. Later that year, Marc got the flu and decided to make one at home, "The Daily Marc." As visitors came and went (that meant anyone who came to the house that week—the mailman and washing machine repairman included), Marc would interview them. If he watched a television show, he would write a review of it. If somebody called him, he would note that call and what that person said. If he completed a homework assignment, he would summarize it in his newspaper. If he finished a book, he would critique it. He would record how he was feeling at different times of the day. Marc also used the paper as a vehicle to thank people who called to see how he was feeling, especially his Grandma Essie and his Grandma Sylvia, the only two people to send him get-well cards (Grandmas are like that). Since Annie has a Xerox machine in her home office, Marc was able to Xerox copies of his newspaper and mail them to all of his friends.

A few months later Annie came across Marc's newspaper sitting in a drawer. What a wonderful diary and memento! What could have been a miserable week in Marc's life was quite a busy and creative experience.

To make your own newspaper, you will need sheets of 8½-by-11-inch paper, pens, pencils, scissors, glue, a typewriter or a computer if you have one, and a stack of 11-by-17-inch paper. Write or type your articles on pieces of 8½-by-11-inch paper. Be sure to write your news stories and articles according to the format of a newspaper column (see drawing and use your local newspaper as a guide). Cut out your columns and paste them onto sheets of 11-by-17-inch paper. Draw pictures or glue photographs onto the 11-by-17-inch sheets to accompany your stories and articles. When you are finished, the pasted-up sheets can be Xeroxed and distributed to family and friends.

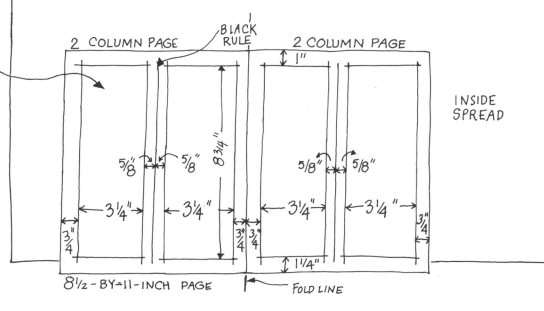

2 COLUMN PAGE

BLACK RULE

2 COLUMN PAGE

1"

INSIDE SPREAD

8¾"

5/8" 5/8"   5/8" 5/8"

|← 3¼" →| |← 3¼" →| |← 3¼" →| |← 3¼" →|

¾"   ¾" ¾"   ¾"

1¼"

8½-BY-11-INCH PAGE

FOLD LINE

The Daily Marc

JANUARY 28TH, 1993 VOL. I

LAUNDRY LEAK!

Washing machine breaks, water goes everywhere. About 1 o'clock the repair man was called to look over the situation.

By 2 o'clock the matter was well in hand and the crisis had passed.

COMIC RELIEF BY MARC

The weather today is rain! RAIN! and more rain!

WEATHER

NEWS UPDATE

Marc is sorry to report he still has the flu with a fever.

BEST ON TV

The new Batman series promises to be as good as everyone hoped.

PHOTO ALBUM

A sick-in-bed day is the perfect time for your child to work on the family "photo album" and to do a little creative writing, too. All you have to do is provide your child with a photo album, a pen, some labels, and, of course, all those photos you've been meaning to organize. As each photo goes into the book, your child writes a caption and puts it under the picture. It can keep him entertained for hours.

♥

Lisa Gilbar's photo albums are unusual in that she likes to include silhouettes and cutout forms in addition to full-framed pictures. In her case, this is a great idea, since many of her pictures have a lot of extra sky.

THE FLIPBOOK

Flipbooks are a wonderful amusement for children of any age. There has been a resurgence of the art and you can find them at a variety of stores. Our illustrator, Jill Weber, has a line of flipbooks and some of our *Penny Whistle* books include flipbooks in them.

You can make a flipbook by following Jill's instructions below. Xerox these drawings or create your own.

YOU WILL NEED
- a small blank notebook, note pad or Post-it pad
- pencil
- markers or crayons

YOU CAN CUT OUT THESE DRAWINGS AND PASTE IN YOUR FLIPBOOK.

YOU CAN TRACE A QUARTER FOR THE CIRCLE OR DRAW FREEHAND.

♥

If you can't find Frajil Farms Flipbooks in your local gift store or bookstore, write to:
Frajil Farms, Inc.
P.O. Box 13
Mont Vernon, NH 03057

HOLD HERE → FLIP HERE ←

MAKE COVER.

DRAW ONLY ON THE RIGHT HALF OF THE PAGE ①

TRY TO KEEP YOUR DRAWINGS IN THE SAME POSITION ON EVERY PAGE.

DO DRAWINGS IN PENCIL FIRST SO YOU CAN ERASE IF THE ACTION DOESN'T WORK.

USE A PUSHPIN TO MARK THE POSITION BY PUSHING THROUGH SEVERAL PAGES.

☆ WE MADE OUR FLIPBOOK 24 PAGES. FOR A LONGER BOOK AND FOR SMOOTHER ACTION, REPEAT EACH DRAWING TWICE (48 PAGES).

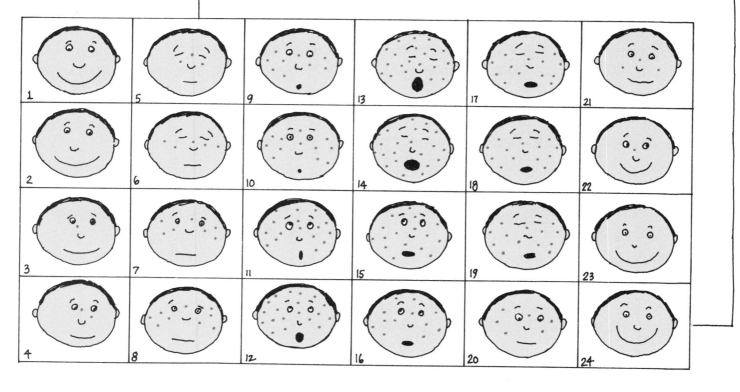

The sound of music can be a natural healer, soothing a cranky child or lifting the mood of a sad one. While he may not feel like singing along, even the sickest child can listen, so make sure to plug in a radio or tape recorder. This is a good time to introduce new styles and artists to your child. Share some of your favorites, too!

MAKE YOUR OWN INSTRUMENTS

The instruments below are easy to make, will last a long time, and will provide hours of "musical" enjoyment for a down-in-the-dumps child.

Drum

Cover an empty coffee can with the plastic lid and turn it upside down. Your child hits the drum with his hands or uses a plastic or wooden spoon as a drumstick.

Coffee Can Shaker

Fill an empty coffee can with beans and cover it with the plastic lid. Tape the lid shut and shake.

Soda Can Shaker

Empty a soda can and pull off the metal tab. Fill it with 1 cup of uncooked rice. Tape over the opening with packing tape and shake.

Milk Bottle Shaker

Take an empty plastic gallon milk bottle and fill it with 3 cups of uncooked popcorn. Close the opening with the bottle cap and shake.

Kazoo

Either buy one or use the old-fashioned method of covering a comb with tissue paper. Show your child how you can hum into the kazoo to make different melodies.

Cymbals

Two metal pot lids banged together make a very satisfying racket.

CRASH

Graters

Rub a wooden spoon back and forth across a plastic grater. This is an effective, although somewhat irritating, noisemaker.

Shoe Box Strummers

Remove the lid from a shoe box and cut a 3-inch hole in the center of the lid. Pull six rubber bands lengthwise around the uncovered box and put the lid back on so that the rubber bands show through the hole. Tape the lid to the box, and presto, a modified guitar!

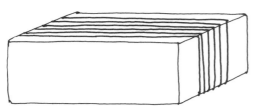

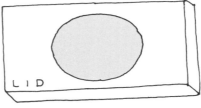

LID

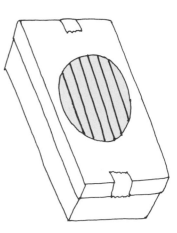

Bells

Available in a multitude of shapes and sizes, bells make wonderful and inexpensive instruments for your home orchestra collection. You can also take a short piece of elastic (big enough for your child's wrist), sew the ends together, and sew on jingle bells for a bell bracelet.

Rhythm Blocks

Take two blocks of wood of the same size and glue a piece of sandpaper to each block. Your child will rub these together with glee (while you may cover your ears!).

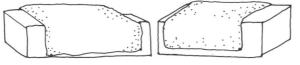

Whistles

These are available at any variety store. To preserve your sanity, buy your child a whistle with a pretty sound (not a shrieking one).

THE GUESSING TAPE

Here's a tape to include in your child's "Sick-Day Box" (see page 31) or to give as a gift to a child that's sick. The point is to play the tape and for your child to guess the sounds.

You will need a cassette tape and a tape recorder. Record a variety of sounds, each lasting at least ten seconds. You can record the sounds of different instruments or familiar sounds like a ticking clock, jingling keys, and a ringing telephone. If you have a second tape recorder, you can record brief sections of familiar songs and play "Name That Tune." You may want to keep a list of the sounds and songs in the order that you recorded them (you may be surprised that it may not be so easy to identify them later!).

MUSIC FOR OLDER CHILDREN

You may have noticed that older children have a more "sophisticated" taste in music and certainly a greater technical expertise than any adult in the household when it comes to all those electronic gadgets. Children ten and over seem very capable of taping music and funny sounds to create their own musical world. Lisa Gilbar, our own queen of the Broadway musicals, often tapes her favorite songs as she sings along. Her friend, Kate Schwab, mixes her own tapes, starring herself as the disc jockey. Her mom, Amy, swears that this is real "get-well therapy."

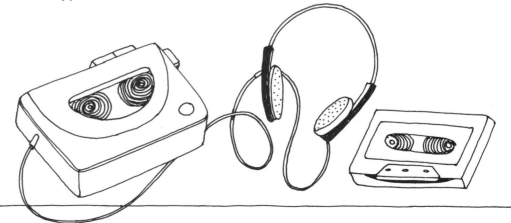

❤
Earphones on your child's tape recorder or radio not only will save the rest of the household from your child's musical taste, but will add to his sense of privacy and allow him to feel alone with his music. It will also give him a sense of control, which he particularly needs when he's not feeling well.

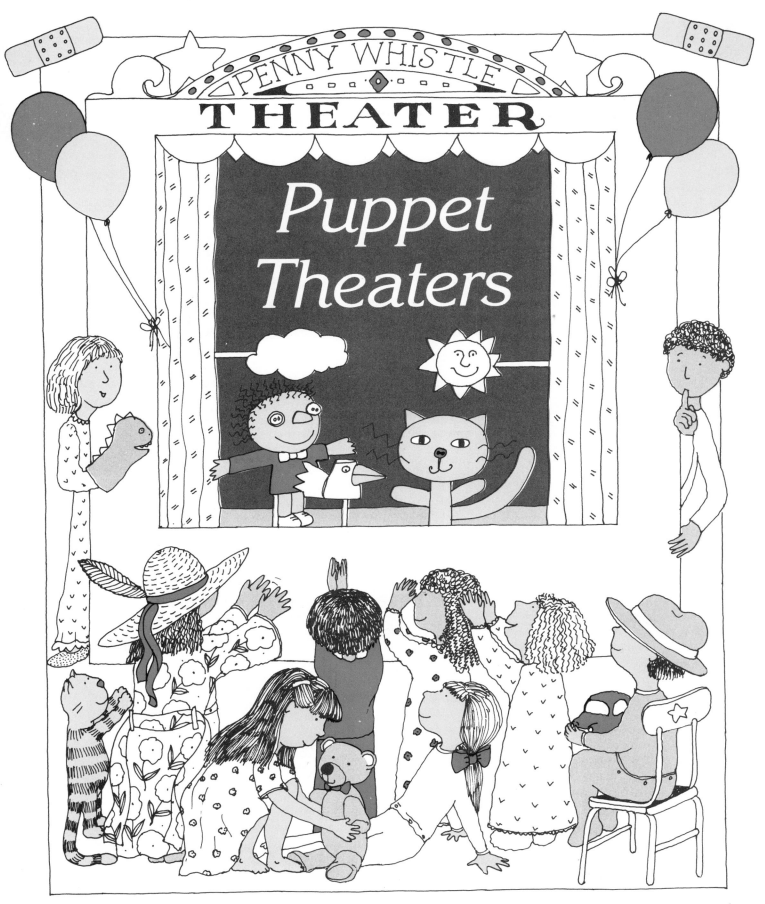

PENNY WHISTLE THEATER

Puppet Theaters

SOUND EFFECTS

CRASH! FILL A CAN WITH BEANS AND SHAKE.

FIRE TAKE A PIECE OF CELLOPHANE AND CRUMBLE IN YOUR HAND.

WIND IF YOU HAVE A WORKING MICROPHONE, BLOW INTO IT.

BELLS RING THE BELLS.

WALKING MARCH HARD WITH HARD-SOLED SHOES.

GALLOPING HORSE SLAP YOUR HANDS ON YOUR KNEES.

TRAIN WHISTLE BLOW A WOODEN WHISTLE.

An ideal way to make time pass when a child is "under the weather" is to engage in the world of make-believe. During those times when real friends can't come over to play, imaginary ones are great substitutes. To enhance these fantasies, pull together some props for play and a collection of puppet-making materials.

Playacting is the best way for children to express their anxiety when they are ill. Explains Dr. Waldstein, "Children like to playact and they also release their fears, frustrations, tensions, and anger by acting out. Such play lets them gain control over their fears. It also gives them a feeling of control over their lives."

While it may not be possible for the child who is ill to get dressed up to play (few children feel like playacting themselves until they are really feeling better), acting through puppets, especially puppets the child made himself, can be part of the healing process. Using puppets gives children permission to act in ways they normally might not by transferring their feelings. A shy child can more easily be raucous, angry, or silly through his puppets, while a self-confident child can really "go to town" or express his vulnerabilities and fears.

Your child can make puppets during the day, then stage a show for the family in the evening.

STRING CURTAIN INSIDE OPENING SO PUPPETEER CAN CONTROL

STA
DOO

PENNY WHISTLE
THEATER

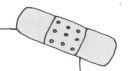

PUPPET THEATER

To make a theater for your puppet show, you will need the largest empty cardboard box you can find. Cut a hole in back of the box large enough to serve as a door for the children. At the front of the box, cut a proscenium square high enough so that the children will not be seen while holding the puppets above their heads. String a curtain across the stage and fasten it to the top of the box so that it hangs down long enough to cover the stage front. You can glue construction paper cut in the shape of scallops around the stage and decorate the "theater" as elaborately as you like.

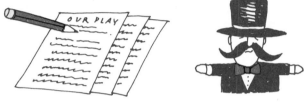

PLAYS

After the puppets have been made, it's time for a show. Encourage dramatizing a familiar simple story, reading lines from a short play, or improvising a script. You can also encourage your child to make up a play, which will give him an opportunity to deal with his feelings about being ill. Try to create a play with a beginning (creating a setting and introducing the characters), a middle (establishing a problem, creating incidents, and/or creating a crisis), and an end (resolving one problem). Some elements to work into a plot include jealousy, a mute puppet, a braggart, jokes (knock-knocks work great), the villain versus the good guy, someone in peril. You could have one puppet tap the other on the head with a club, crush soda crackers to make a mess, do magic tricks, use disguises, make weather changes (storms, make lightning with flashlights, thunder, snow with confetti).

Use props like miniature hats, toys, cars, and buses. Include background music, if possible. Plan a rehearsal and schedule a performance for friends and family.

♥
A miniature hospital (like a doll's house) with patient rooms, an X-ray area, labs, a treatment room, an operating room, a kitchen, a bathroom, and a playroom becomes an excellent "stage" for your child's playacting.

♥
"The Doctor's Bag" (see page 23) is a useful prop for medical dramatics. On a sheet on the bed table, place a doll or a stuffed animal, a few instruments, and some "hospital" clothing.

PUPPETS TO MAKE

If you're looking for an inexpensive yet entertaining puppet project, gather those odds and ends that have collected in drawers, boxes, cupboards, and closets. Add to them any other items, such as scraps of cloth, yarn, beads, buttons, dried macaroni, beans, corn kernels, ribbon, cotton balls, marshmallows, and bottle caps. You will also need scissors, crayons, markers, glue, construction paper, brown paper lunch bags and the larger grocery sacks, stiff cardboard, paper towel tubes, a stapler, and paint and brushes.

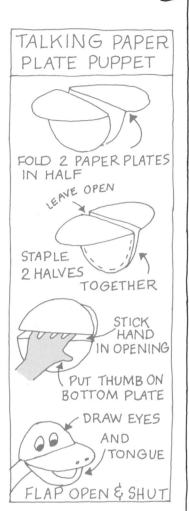

TALKING PAPER
PLATE PUPPET

FOLD 2 PAPER PLATES
IN HALF

LEAVE OPEN

STAPLE
2 HALVES
TOGETHER

STICK
HAND
IN OPENING

PUT THUMB ON
BOTTOM PLATE

DRAW EYES
AND
TONGUE

FLAP OPEN & SHUT

♥

For cups and plates with waxy, paint-resistant surfaces, mix a small amount of liquid dishwashing detergent or Future floor wax with tempera paint so that the paint will adhere smoothly.

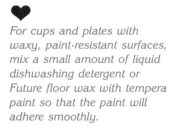

PAPER CUP PUPPET

PAPER PLATE PUPPETS

An easy puppet to make is the "paper plate puppet." Because of both their texture and shape, paper plates can easily be turned into animals, people, and objects.

Collect paper plates both small and large and in assorted colors. You can also use special-purpose paper plates like soup bowls, oval plates, or plates with dividers. Your supplies should include a small stapler, a tube of roll-on glue, crayons or markers, scissors, Popsicle sticks, drinking straws, egg cartons, paper towel tubes, and scraps of fabric.

To make a paper plate puppet, staple two paper plates together around the outer edges, leaving enough space to insert a paper towel tube between the plates. Glue the plates to the tube. You can cut the plates into any shape and decorate to create any character you like.

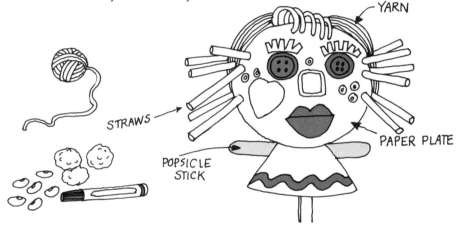

YARN

STRAWS

POPSICLE
STICK

PAPER PLATE

PAPER CUP PUPPETS

Paper cups come in a variety of shapes and sizes—and so do puppets! Search the stores for cone cups, mini cups, Styrofoam cups, cups with handles, and add these to your resource collection for puppet making. Children enjoy combining and stacking cups in different ways to create characters, and they also find them useful for building features onto other puppets.

Attach a wooden Popsicle stick to the inside of a cup. When you move the stick your puppet moves, too.

CUT
OUT

MAKE SLIT

CONE
CUP

CUT TOP OF
PAPER CUP

ATTACH
TO STICK

STAPLE
OR GLUE

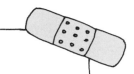

PAPER BAG PUPPETS

This project lends itself to younger ages. Let your child use his imagination to create the puppet faces. Suggest making a clown, an animal, or a monster to help him get started. He can use yarn for hair, cotton for a beard, dried beans for teeth, buttons or bottle caps for eyes, and scraps of fabric for clothing. Doilies make shirt collars. Leftover Christmas wrapping paper makes excellent clown attire.

You will need brown paper lunch bags and larger grocery bags, markers, and odds and ends.

The bag can be used in two basic ways to create the puppet's head: The bottom flap of the bag can act as the top lip while the bottom lip is drawn on the bag itself where the top flap meets it. The flap of the bag can then be manipulated to simulate lip movement as the puppeteer speaks and makes his puppet "talk." Or, the flap can have eyelids drawn on it instead of lips, with the eyes depicted on the bag where the flap meets.

Make puppet clothes with Velcro so they can easily be removed and switched from puppet to puppet. (You can also use Velcro for closing your child's clothes that need to be removed easily or quickly!)

FLAP UP

FLAP DOWN

SPOON PUPPETS

These puppets are made quickly and easily and are ready for a show immediately, which is a big plus for younger children.

You will need wooden spoons of various shapes and sizes, markers, beads, yarn, and cotton balls.

Using markers, paint faces on the wooden spoons. Encourage your child to create faces with different expressions and remember to include things like hair, mustaches, ears, glasses, even a collar or two. Of course, it's possible to create more elaborate spoon characters by gluing on beads, yarn, cotton balls, raffia, and fabric, as well.

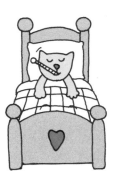

SHADOW PUPPETS

These puppets perform *behind* the curtain! You will need pieces of thin card-board (laundry inserts from men's shirts are perfect), scissors, thin sticks 1½ to 2 inches long, pushpins, a screen (see instructions below), a shaded lamp or spotlight, and scenery.

For each puppet, draw an outline of a fun, fanciful, weird, crazy, or lifelike character on a piece of cardboard (imagination is everything here). Cut out the figure. Use a pushpin to attach the cardboard figure to a thin stick.

To make a screen, you will need a frame of stiff cardboard approximately 2½ by 3 feet (see drawing). Stretch a piece of unbleached muslin across the front of the frame and attach it to the sides of the frame with a staple gun. Set the screen on two chairs—positioned at opposite ends of the screen—and tie it in place with string. Place a shaded lamp or spotlight somewhere at the top of and behind the screen so that the puppets' shadows will be projected onto the screen (you can also use colored theatrical gels in front of the light source and experiment with lighting effects). Tape or pin cutout paper scenery—grass, trees, clouds, flowers, houses—onto the muslin, but leave a large enough area for the puppets to perform. Cover the area below the screen with a cloth so that the puppeteer won't be visible.

Now darken the room and you're ready to perform!

Toe puppets placed on the toes of someone with a foot cast will encourage wiggling and be a fun form of exercise for the toes.

LIGHT BEHIND THE SCREEN

← STICK

CARDBOARD FRAME

STAPLE MUSLIN ACROSS FRAME

TIE TO CHAIR

COVER THIS AREA WITH A CLOTH

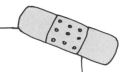

FLASHLIGHT PUPPETS

You will need brown paper lunch bags, markers, scissors, masking tape, flash-lights, dark tempera paint, glue, cardboard, an X-acto knife, plastic wrap, Scotch tape, and colored tissue paper or cellophane.

Make at least two puppets so they can have a "conversation." First, draw a face on the side of each bag. Next, color in the features with simple bold lines; cut out the eyes. Slip the bag over a flashlight and tighten the "neck" with masking tape (allowing room to operate the on/off switch). Darken the room to heighten the effect of the lighted puppet as it dances and moves about. Scene changes and puppet entrances and exits are facilitated by switching the flash-lights on and off.

For a spookier effect, paint the outside of the bag completely with dark tempera paint. When the bag is dry, glue a piece of cardboard inside to create a stiff surface. Draw in the features, then use an X-acto knife to carefully cut them out. To make the pupils float in the eye sockets, paint the pupils on plastic wrap and then position the wrap behind the cutout sockets. Secure with Scotch tape. The plastic can be moved, producing different expressions.

The eyes and other cutout facial features can also be covered with colored tissue paper or cellophane to produce special lighting effects.

♥ *Try taping colored cellophane lollipop wrappers over the flashlight lenses.*

HAND PUPPET

♥ *You can pull a "filmstrip" of eyeballs through slits in a mask and animate a still face.*

♥ *Accessorize the puppets with items such as hats, ties, shoes, purses and wallets, and lots of jewelry.*

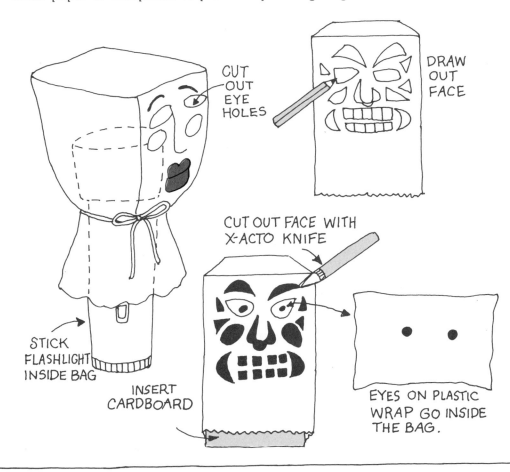

CUT OUT EYE HOLES

DRAW OUT FACE

STICK FLASHLIGHT INSIDE BAG

INSERT CARDBOARD

CUT OUT FACE WITH X-ACTO KNIFE

EYES ON PLASTIC WRAP GO INSIDE THE BAG.

Use an old white glove (painter's or gardener's gloves work great—and they are not expensive!) to make finger puppets by painting a face on each finger. The whole glove can be worn or the fingers of the glove can be cut off, to the length of the child's fingers, and slipped on the child's fingers separately.

Turn peanut shells into wonderful finger puppets. Make a cap for each finger from peanut shell halves. Draw the faces with ink. Finger puppets are especially good for a child whose hands are not strong.

GLOVE PUPPETS

This is really a simple way of making instant puppets.

You will need a pair of old knitted gloves, scissors, felt, glue, paint, a paintbrush, yarn, and fabric scraps.

Take each glove, stick your hand in it, and let your fingers do the walking. Your pointer and middle fingers can be the legs, with your pinkie and thumb acting as the arms. You can cut a head out of felt and glue it onto the back of the glove. Make whiskers out of the hairs from a paintbrush, paint lips on with tempera paint, or decorate as you wish using buttons, yarn, fabric, and other materials.

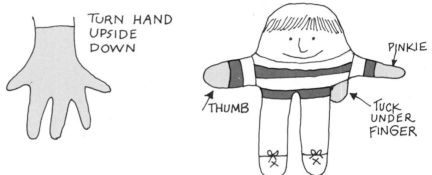

FINGER PUPPETS

"Finger puppets" are particularly appealing because they are easy to make and are a size appropriate for young children.

You will need pieces of felt, a needle and thread or glue, and a hole punch.

To make a simple finger puppet, use your child's finger as a pattern around which you wrap a small piece of felt, about 3 by 4 inches, depending on the size of your child's finger. Stitch or glue the seams. Use a hole punch to make eyes or glue on plastic eyes or beads. Add small beads, tassels, sequins, ribbon, yarn, and other materials and create a cat, a clown, a king, a queen, a monkey, or any other character.

STICK PUPPETS

Another kind of puppet is the "stick puppet," which is merely a stick with a painted and decorated cardboard head on it.

Games

♥

When Remy Weber was five he had a Snoopy doll and a large collection of outfits for it. Whenever Remy was sick Jill found Snoopy wearing an outfit that seemed to fit Remy's mood. One day Snoopy was in his surgical greens, with a face mask on. Another day he wore his zip-up sleeper, and another day he looked ready to take on the world in his blue jeans. After a while, Jill could tell how Remy was feeling by Snoopy's ensemble.

Playing games helps to pass the time for a sick child. It can take his mind away from the illness and challenge and engage him in a positive and entertaining way.

In this section you will find over thirty games that will keep your child happily occupied. Next to each game you will find the suggested ages (but keep in mind that a child who is not feeling well may be more inclined to play games that you would normally think are too easy for him or not "age appropriate") and we are repeating our symbols: A little bed means this game can be played in bed and it is perfect for children who may be temporarily immobilized. All other games can be played when your child is feeling a little better and is not confined to his bed. One smiling face means this game can be played with one person; two smiling faces means this game needs two or more players. A gift-wrapped box means that this activity is a "kit."

We begin with a list of the perfect bed games: travel games. These miniature magnetic board games are great for playing in bed because the pieces can be tilted and jiggled and will not fall off the bed. They can be found at any well-stocked toy store.

BACKGAMMON (Pressman)

CHECKERS / CHESS (Pressman)

CLUE (Parker Brothers)

MONOPOLY, JR. (Parker Brothers)

PERIL (Pressman)

POCKET SIMON (Milton Bradley)

SORRY! (Parker Brothers)

TRAVEL BATTLESHIP (Milton Bradley)

TRAVEL CHINESE CHECKERS (Pressman)

TRAVEL CONNECT FOUR (Milton Bradley)

TRAVEL LABYRINTH (Cardinal)

TRAVEL MAGNA DOODLE (Tyco)

TRAVEL MASTERMIND (Pressman)

TRAVEL PERFECTION (Milton Bradley)

TRAVEL SCRABBLE (Milton Bradley)

TRAVEL SHARK ATTACK (Milton Bradley)

TRAVEL TROUBLE (Milton Bradley)

TRAVEL YAHTZEE (Milton Bradley)

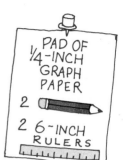

SHIPS AT SEA

This game works best with two players. You will need a pad of ¼-inch graph paper, two pencils, and two 6-inch rulers. First you must make your game sheets (see drawing): For each sheet, draw a box measuring 10 squares by 10 squares at the top of the page. Repeat at the bottom of the page. Write the numbers 1 through 10 above each square in the top line. Write the letters A through J beside each square in the first vertical line. Repeat in the box below. Label the top box "Mine"; the bottom box, "The Enemy." If you have access to a copying machine, you can draw a master game sheet and run off a stack of copies.

To play, each person takes a game sheet and in the box marked "Mine" hides the four different kinds of ships in straight lines, up and down or across, in random spots. (See drawing: The battleship occupies five squares, the cruiser is four, the destroyer is three, and the submarine is two.) Label your ships. Don't allow your opponent to see your sheet. He will be attempting to guess where you've hidden your ships, while you are trying to find his ships. The players take turns calling out coordinates. If your opponent calls "F7," you put an *X* in square "F7" in the "Mine" box. If your opponent hits one of your ships, you must tell your opponent he has a hit and he will put an *X* in square "F7" in his "Enemy" box.

Now it is your turn. You may say, "A2." If your opponent tells you you have a hit, put an *X* in square "A2" in your "Enemy" box; he will put an *X* in "A2" in his "Mine" box. As all the ships have been placed horizontally and vertically, you will know that you should hit up and down, to the right or left of a square, until you "sink" one of his ships. A player wins when he has destroyed all of his opponent's ships.

(Ages 8 and up)

BATTLESHIP
5 BOXES

CRUISER
4 BOXES

DESTROYER
3 BOXES

SUBMARINE
2 BOXES

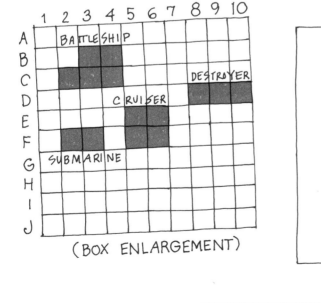

(BOX ENLARGEMENT)

MINE

ENEMY

8½-by-11 inches

84

STACK OF PAPER
AND RULER
OR
GRAPH PAPER

PENCILS

S	L	S	N
H	O	E	I
O	V	E	N
E	E	M	E

THE WORDSMITH GAME

Here's a game that will give your child's vocabulary a workout. It is a little like Scrabble, and can be played with as many people as you like or just with two. Each player has a game sheet on which you have drawn a box 5 squares by 5 squares (if your child can write very small legible letters, try using graph paper, marking off a large box so there will be a finite number of squares for the letters). The first player calls out any letter of the alphabet. Each player writes in the letter anywhere he wants to on his game sheet. Then the next player calls out a letter, and the players put it down anywhere. The object is to build as many words as possible from the letters, going up and down or across but not on the diagonal. The game continues, each player calling out a letter, until all the squares are filled. The player using the most letters to form words is the winner. (For kids over twelve, you can make the game more challenging by making more or fewer squares, or by permitting words on the diagonal as well as up and down and across.)

A variation of this is "Foursomes." Each player gets a game sheet on which you have drawn a box 4 squares by 4 squares. The first player calls out any letter he likes. All the players write it down in any one of the sixteen squares. The second player calls out a letter, and so on, until sixteen letters have been called. The object of the game is to put the letters in the squares in such a way that they form four-letter words. The player with the most words wins. Words may be formed across, diagonally, or up and down.

(Ages 7 and up)

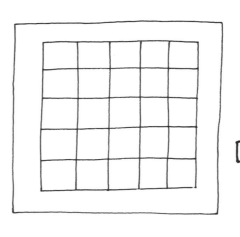

CENTER OF ATTENTION

You will need a large colorful poster or picture. Hang the poster or the picture on the wall opposite the bed and darken the room. Use a flashlight to spotlight all the things that are alike. For example: all the plants, all the animals, or all the buildings.

(Ages 3 and up)

PENNY PITCH

Lean a muffin pan against the wall or at the end of the bed so the top edge of the pan rests at an angle. Assign a point value to each cup. Have your child sit as far away as possible on the bed or play from a lying position. Just make sure the pan is completely visible.

Start with three pennies. Calculate the score by adding up the point values of the muffin cups that have pennies in them. Two or more players should take turns throwing or tossing three pennies at a time. The object is to keep trying to better your score or beat your opponent if you have one.

(Ages 5 and up)

MUFFIN PAN
THREE PENNIES
PEN AND PAD

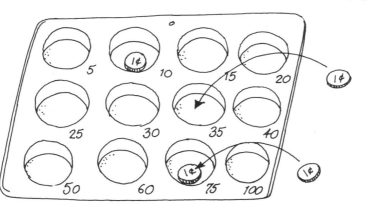

SEARCH ME

Collect a pile of old magazines and catalogs and give your child different challenges. The first might be to have your child find as many items as he can in a particular color or in different shades of that color. These items can then be cut out and pasted onto a large piece of foam board for display. Another time have him cut out pictures of cars, dogs, or favorite foods. You can turn it into a contest between you and your child. This also works as an activity for your child to do with visitors.

(Ages 4 and up)

You can make a felt cover or quilt made out of alternating squares, like a tic-tac-toe board. Use stuffed animals as the game pieces.

OLD MAGAZINES
& CATALOGS
SCISSORS
GLUE
PAPER

TWENTY PAIRS OF
PHOTOS
OR
SCISSORS
MAGAZINES
GLUE

POSTER BOARD
OR
FOAM BOARD

MEMORIES

This game requires approximately twenty pairs of pictures. Any kind of pictures will do: When Lisa Gilbar was out of school with the flu for a week, Gary, her dad, took one roll of twenty-four photos of different recognizable items from the streets of Los Angeles including famous street signs, interesting cars and people, palm trees, Lisa's school and playground, and even a couple of her friends. He had them developed at a drugstore that promised "two shots for the price of one." If you prefer, you can cut twenty pictures out of a magazine and paste them onto pieces of poster board or foam board. Cut them in half.

To play the game, mix up the pictures and place them face down on a hard surface. Then, either alone or with another person, your child must pick matching pairs or halves. When your child finds a pair, he keeps it. If he doesn't pick a pair, he puts the pictures back in the same spot on the table, face down, trying to remember where they are placed. As the game progresses, your child will get to see most of the pictures and it will be easier for him to remember where the pairs are.

This game can also be played with a regular deck of playing cards.

(Ages 4 and up)

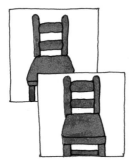

BALL GAMES

Sponge ball games made to be played indoors are perfect for an athlete stuck at home. Look for sponge golf balls, tennis balls, Ping-Pong (floor) balls, footballs, and basketballs.

One of our favorites is "Follow the Bouncing Ball." Place an egg carton on the floor. From a line 6 to 8 feet away, bounce a sponge ball (or use a Ping-Pong ball) on the floor and try to get it into the carton. To score, the ball must remain in one of the compartments. Your child can play alone or with visitors. If more than one person is playing, each player has three attempts each turn, and each time the ball remains in the carton he scores one point.

(Ages 5 and up)

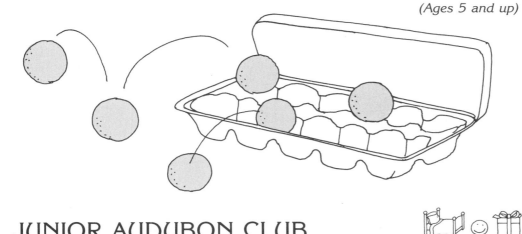

SPONGE
PING-PONG
BALLS,
FOOTBALLS,
AND BASKETBALLS
EGG CARTON
PENCIL
SCORE PAD

♥
Jason Bloom suggests that you spread bird feed outside your child's window to attract many birds.

BIRD BOOK
(FOR IDENTIFICATION)
MARKERS

BINOCULARS
(REAL OR
PRETEND)

PENCIL

NOTEBOOK

JUNIOR AUDUBON CLUB

Young children often think of birds as friends. If your child is a bird-watcher in the making, he may enjoy looking for his little friends more than ever while he is stuck in bed. You will need a paperback bird identification book (the Golden Book series is good and inexpensive [check your local library or bookstore]), markers, a notebook, and binoculars (real or pretend). Your child can watch for birds from his window and try to match the birds he sees to their pictures in the book. He can put an *X* beside each picture or record the bird's name in his own notebook as real bird-watchers do. From time to time have him count his *X*'s to see how many birds he has spotted! This is also a great way to learn the name of the bird if it is new to him.

(Ages 4 and up)

ALL MIXED-UP PUZZLES

Collect old photos or magazine pictures of people and six small (1½ by 1½ inches square) cardboard boxes. If your toy chest has old square blocks that can be donated to this project, use them instead of the boxes; craft stores often sell blocks of different sizes. Remember, the pictures should all be approximately the same size and large enough to cover the sides of the boxes or blocks when cut up.

Choose photos of six different people and cut each photo into six parts. Now paste the pieces onto the boxes or blocks with each box or block displaying one part of each person on each of its six sides.

To play the game, the boxes or blocks are mixed up and your child has to reassemble the pieces to get a proper portrait. You will need a hard surface to work on to do this in bed. Actually, this isn't a very difficult puzzle, as puzzles go, and the fun is in combining the various body parts in odd ways (such as one person's nose with another's chin).

For a variation of this game, use pictures of animals or cartoon characters. Or combine animals and people and see how many silly new creations your child can come up with.

(Ages 3 and up)

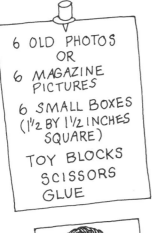

6 OLD PHOTOS
OR
6 MAGAZINE
PICTURES
6 SMALL BOXES
(1½ BY 1½ INCHES
SQUARE)
TOY BLOCKS
SCISSORS
GLUE

CUT PICTURES INTO 6 PARTS

PASTE ONE SQUARE
ON EACH SIDE OF BLOCK

CONNECTIONS

You may recognize this game as the long-lived doodle game most grandmas and grandpas remember playing as children. The reason that it has stood the test of time is that it's an easy way to pass the time. You'll find it a particularly good game to recommend to a child not feeling well.

To play, take a piece of graph paper. Use one sheet for each game, no matter how many players are involved. Draw dots to form squares (see drawing). Each player takes a turn drawing a line between the dots. When a player completes a square, he writes his initial in it so he knows it's his. A player who completes a square gets to go again. (This means that he can sometimes complete several squares, one after another.) When all the dots are connected, the person with the most squares wins.

For a variation, you can make this "Five in a Row." The object is for each player to get five of his boxes in a row, up and down, across, or diagonally. Each player in turn tries to block the others from getting five in a row.

(Ages 5 and up)

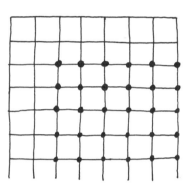

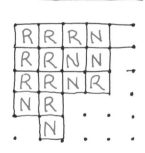

Ronna Gordon plays this game with toothpicks. Instead of drawing a line, you put a toothpick between the dots. (The dots will have to be farther apart so that the toothpicks will fit between them properly.) Then, instead of putting his initial in the square, each player can place a different color poker chip in his square to indicate ownership.

SQUIGGLES AND WIGGLES

Begin by drawing a short wiggly line on a piece of paper. Your child must study the line and make some kind of drawing out of it. You will find that you can make figures, animals, houses, or anything else by turning the paper sideways, upside down, or any other way. If more than two people play, each makes a wiggly line on his paper and then gives it to the player next to him for that player to use as his starting point.

(Ages 4 and up)

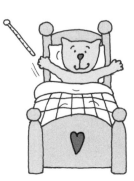

2 PENCILS

MASKING TAPE

PAPER

THE SHADOW

Double writing is fun to experiment with, and you can also use it to make interesting designs. Fasten two pencils together with a piece of masking tape, pulling one pencil up a little so the tips are not even. Both pencils can be black or they can be different colors. Now hold the pencils so both points will touch the paper at the same time. Write the way you usually do, but this time you will create two sets of words, one beneath the other. You can write messages, stories, or create wonderful drawings!

(All ages)

COIN CHECKERS

This game is for two players. On a piece of paper, draw a box made up of sixteen squares: four rows of four squares each. Take four nickels and four pennies and arrange them on the playing board as shown: nickel, penny, nickel, penny. One player moves the pennies and the other moves the nickels.

The players take turns moving one coin in any direction, but only one square at a time. You can go up and down, side to side, or on the diagonal. There is no "jumping" over any coins (as there is in real checkers) and two coins can't be on the same square. The winner is the first player to get all four of his coins in a straight line.

(Ages 6 and up)

PAPER
RULER

4 5¢ NICKELS

4 1¢ PENNIES

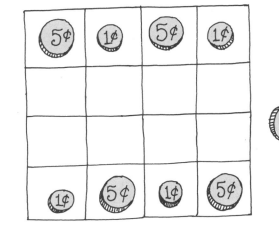

KALAH

(This is also called "Mancala," the African bead game. It is sold in many toy stores.)

"Kalah" is a game of skill that some people say is at least seven thousand years old. It can be enjoyed by children and adults (Annie learned it on a trip to Israel when she was only eight and still likes to play). You will need an egg carton for the playing board and thirty-six markers (they can be pennies, beans, or—Annie's favorite—buttons, or a combination of these). In learning the rules, it will be helpful to refer to the illustration. The players sit on opposite sides of the game board. The six egg cups on each player's side belong to him, and the table space to the right of each player's side of the board is his "Kalah." The object of the game is to see which player can collect the most markers in his own Kalah.

The degree of difficulty depends on the number of buttons in each cup at the start of play. For beginners, both players put three buttons in each of the six cups on his side. One player goes first and picks up all the buttons in any one of his six cups, and then puts those buttons, one by one, in each cup, moving around the board to his right. If he reaches the last cup on his side of the board and still has buttons left in his hand, he puts one button in his Kalah space and continues counterclockwise, putting buttons, one by one, in his opponent's cups. However, a player never puts any buttons in his opponent's Kalah. If the last button of a player's move lands in his own Kalah, he gets another turn. If the last button of a player's move lands in an empty cup on his own side of the board, he then takes all the buttons out of his opponent's cup directly opposite his own empty cup. He puts these buttons into his own Kalah, together with the button used to capture them. That ends that player's move.

The game is over when all six cups on either player's side are empty. Then the player whose cups are not empty takes all the buttons remaining in his own cups and puts them into his Kalah. The players then count up the buttons and the one with the most in his Kalah is the winner.

(Ages 7 and up)

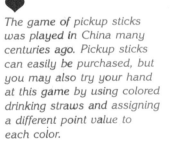

EGG CARTON

36 MARKERS

The game of pickup sticks was played in China many centuries ago. Pickup sticks can easily be purchased, but you may also try your hand at this game by using colored drinking straws and assigning a different point value to each color.

CUT OFF TOP OF EGG CARTON

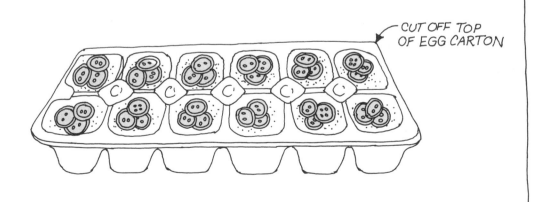

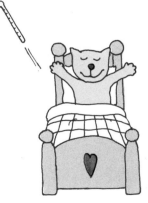

TWIN NUMBER MAZE

All you need for this game is a pencil and paper. On a large sheet of paper, write the numbers 1 through 20 so that they are randomly scattered. Now write the numbers 1 through 20 again all over the paper trying not to have matching numbers near each other. (To make an alphabet maze, use the letters A through Z in place of numbers.)

The object of the game is to connect the duplicate numbers (or letters) with pencil lines without touching or crossing another line. Each player in turn connects two matching numbers with a line, starting with the 1's and proceeding in order through the 20's. You don't have to draw the shortest route between two numbers. If you want to mess up the other player's track, just draw a long, winding line. Usually the game begins to get tough when you reach the mid-teens. The first player who can't connect two matching numbers without his line touching or crossing another line loses.

(Ages 5 and up)

HINT: ☆
CIRCLE THE NUMBERS AS YOU CONNECT THEM.

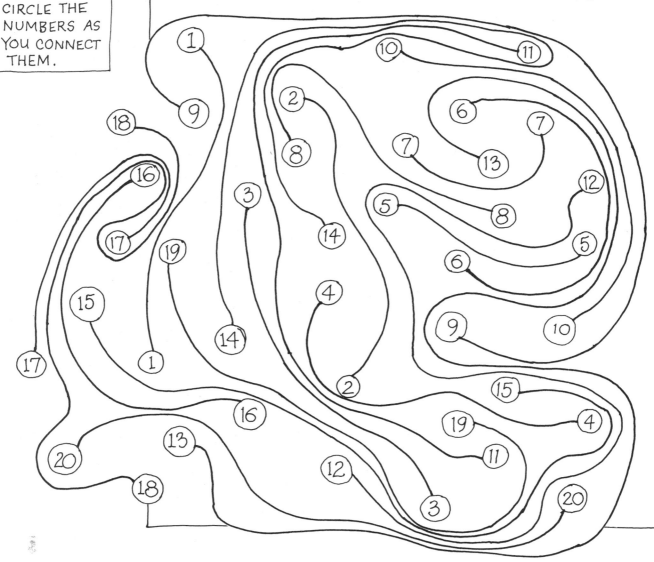

DON'T CROSS ME

The first player draws a house and surrounds it with twelve to twenty dots. The second player shows him what dot to circle. The first player starts from the chimney and draws a line circling the dot. The second player carries the line from the circled dot to the next one indicated by the first player, and so on, until all the dots are circled. The player with the last turn then must take the line back to the chimney. All this must be done without touching or crossing any lines.

(Ages 8 and up)

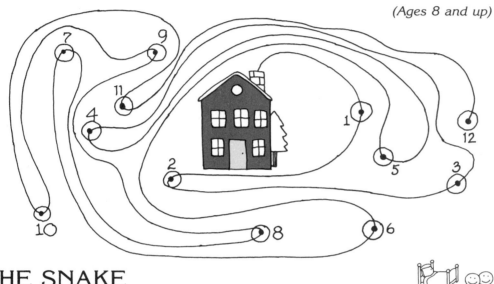

THE SNAKE

To begin, mark ten rows of ten dots each on a sheet of paper. The first player draws a horizontal or vertical line to join any two adjacent dots; diagonal lines are not allowed. The second player then draws another line, connecting either end of the existing line horizontally or vertically to any adjacent dot. The players then continue playing alternately in this manner, drawing a line from either end of the existing line ("the snake") to an adjacent dot. The object is to force your opponent into a position in which he has to draw a line that will connect either end of the snake back to itself, thus causing him to lose the game.

(Ages 6 and up)

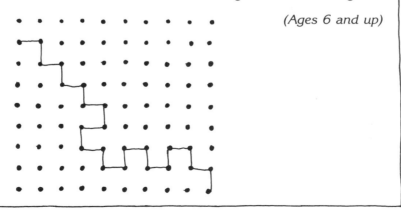

PAPER

PENCILS

TAXI!

On a sheet of paper, write the numbers 1 through 21 in random order in three parallel lines across the page, each line of numbers representing a street and each number a house. In the upper left-hand corner, draw a little square for the garage of the taxi driver. One player is the taxi driver and the other is the passenger. The passenger directs the driver to take him to a house, say, number 11 on First Street. The driver must draw a line from the garage to house number 11. The passenger may then say, "Drive me to 6 Third Street," and the driver draws a line from number 11 to number 6, but must not cross the previous line (the passenger may call any house number that he chooses, but may go to each house only once). This goes on until the driver can't go to the address asked for without crossing one of his previous lines. His turn as taxi driver then ends, and he counts the number of houses that he has visited; that is his score.

The players then change roles for a new diagram, and the one who was the driver becomes the passenger and vice versa. The driver who has visited the most houses is the winner. Your child can also play alone by calling out his own numbers.

(Ages 6 and up)

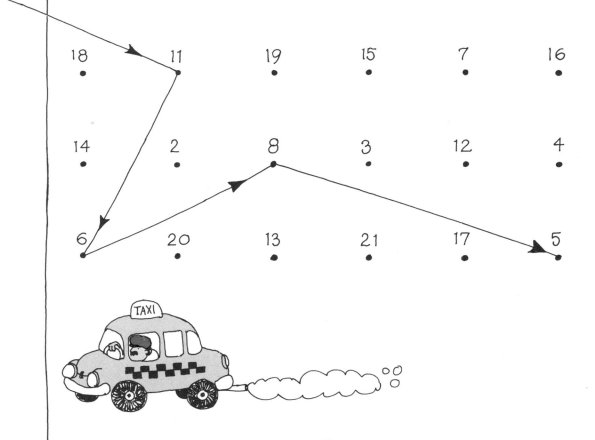

SCRAMBLE

Buy a deck of flash cards with the letters of the alphabet on them at the toy store. There will be a card for each letter of the alphabet, with about six cards each for the letters most commonly used. You can make your own set of cards if you prefer.

To play, mix up all the cards and divide them between two players, face down on a hard surface. The first player picks a letter from his pile and lays it face up to form a row. The second player does the same. As soon as either player can make a word out of one of the letters he has turned over *and* the letters laid down by the other player, he gets to pick up all of his cards and the cards he used from the other player. After a while, the player with the most words has the most cards, too. Keep track of the words each player makes.

(Ages 8 and up)

ROULETTE

Set up a roulette wheel. You can teach your child how to bet with odds on the board and to choose how many chips he wants to place on the numbers. Some children prefer just to bet on the colors red and black, or on even and odd numbers (in this way it is easy to tell who won and how much they won). Games of chance are entertaining and it is fun to have visitors participate in the game.

(Ages 6 and up)

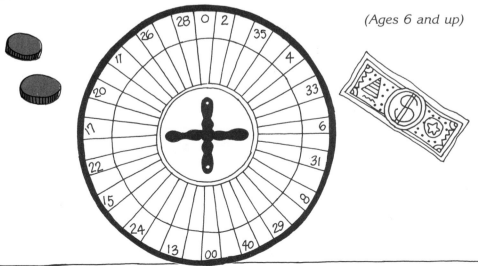

DECK OF ALPHABET CARDS

PENCIL

PAD OF PAPER

♥

Young, budding investors can easily follow the stock market. Marc Gilbar first did this when he got the flu and had to miss school when his fifth-grade class was studying the stock market as a math exercise. Marc "invested" a pretend amount of money in certain stocks and then watched those stocks in the newspaper to see how he did. Jeff Buhai tried the same thing. "Some of my stocks went up and on some of them I lost. But the most fun was being able to watch what was happening in the paper every day."

ROULETTE WHEEL

RED &
BLACK
POKER CHIPS

CARDS
PENCIL & PAPER

CRAZY EIGHTS

Two to four can play this game. You will need a deck of cards and a pencil and paper to keep score. The object is to be the first to get rid of all your cards. It's a great card game to play in bed because the cards can be piled up so that they don't slide around on your bed tray.

One person is the dealer. If two people are playing, each gets seven cards; if three or four are playing, each person gets five cards. Put the rest of the deck face down in a pile. Turn the top card up and place it beside the pile to start the discard pile. The players take turns putting single cards from their hands down onto the discard pile. A card can be placed on the discard pile if it matches the suit or the rank of the top card; for example, the six of clubs can go on top of the three of clubs, and the six of clubs can be followed by the six of diamonds. All eights are "wild" and can be substituted for any other card; an eight can also be discarded on top of any other discard. The beauty of getting an eight is that when you play it you can then choose any suit you want for the next card (the next player has to follow with the suit you named or with another eight). When you can't match the previous card in suit or rank, you must draw cards from the stock until you can, and then discard to complete your turn. (You can, if you want, draw from the stock even if you already have a valid play—perhaps to save an eight in your hand in case of an emergency.)

The first player to get rid of all of his cards is the winner. If the stock is finished and no one can throw a card from his hand, the game is "blocked," and the player with the fewest cards in his hand is the winner.

When the Gilbars play this game, they keep score. In their version, after you win, you get the points for the cards that are left in the other players' hands: 50 points for each eight, 10 points for each face card, 1 point for each ace, and the real value of each of all the other cards (7 points for a seven, etc.). The first player to reach 100 points (or any other goal you determine) is the winner.

(Ages 8 and up)

EITHER ① ② OR ③ COULD B THE FIRST MOVE

① ② ③

WILD CARD

FIRST PLAYER

SLAPJACK

You will need a standard deck of cards. The object is to get all the cards in the deck. The players divide the cards evenly among them. If the players are too young to know how to deal, they can take turns pulling single cards from the deck, or the deck can simply be divided into approximately equal-size stacks. Players keep their cards in face-down stacks in front of them; no peeking allowed.

Starting with the first player, each person takes turns throwing his top card onto a face-up pile in the center of the circle. Whenever a jack is turned over, the players race to slap it with their hands. Whoever hits the jack first gets the whole pile of cards underneath, and adds them face down to the bottom of his own stack. If a player accidentally slaps a card that isn't a jack, he has to pay a penalty by giving one of his cards to the player who took the last turn.

A player who loses all of his cards has only one chance to get back in the game: by slapping the jack the next time it appears. If he manages this successfully, he is back in the game with the pile he slapped; otherwise he is out permanently.

The winner of the game is the one who collects all the cards. Or, to keep the game from taking too long, the game may end the first time a player goes out of the game, with the one who has the most cards at that point declared the winner.

(Ages 4 and up)

Why not gather various travel brochures from a travel agent and encourage your child to pretend to go to different places in his imagination?

98

KLONDIKE

CARDS

This is the classic game of solitaire. The instructions seem difficult, but once learned it is a card game that many enjoy playing for long stretches of time. It would be a bonus to learn from a seasoned card player!

This game is played alone with a regular deck of cards. The object is to complete piles in suits and in number sequence. Deal out a row of seven cards from left to right, the first face up, the rest face down. Then deal a card face up on top of the second card, followed by single face-down cards on each of the remaining cards to the right. Follow this with a face-up card on what is now the third pile and face-down cards on the piles to its right. Continue this pattern until you have a row of seven piles, each with one more card than the one before it, with the top card of each pile face up and the ones below all face down.

This is the tableau. The remaining cards form the hand. Cards are turned over from the hand three at a time. Only the last card is looked at.

As aces become available during the game, either by appearing as the hand is turned or as top cards in the tableau piles, place them in a row above the tableau to begin the foundations. Deal three cards from the hand, look at the third, make all possible moves, then deal three again. To win the game, you must build the four ace foundations all the way up, in sequence and in the same suit. The top cards of the tableau piles are always available to be built onto a foundation pile.

BEGINNING GAME

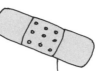

During the game, you can place a card from the hand on a tableau pile if the top card is of next-higher rank and opposite color. It is also possible to move a lone tableau card or an entire sequence of cards from one tableau pile to another, provided that all the face-up cards on the transferred tableau pile are moved as a unit; portions of sequences cannot be moved. When building within the tableau or from tableau to foundation exposes a face-down tableau card, the card is turned over.

Any spaces formed in the tableau row can be filled by kings. After all four kings have been used to fill spaces, any card can be placed in an available gap.

To use cards in the hand, turn the cards over in packets of three at a time, and put them face up. This is the talon pile. The top card from each packet of three is available for building on the tableau or foundations. If it is used, the next card in the packet becomes available. After running through the hand once in packets of three, the hand is turned over and the process starts again. The game is lost if you have run through the hand once or twice without being able to make any more plays.

In a somewhat more difficult version of "Klondike," the hand is run through one card at a time, but it can be used only once. The game is lost if the hand is run through and there are no more available plays.

(Ages 8 and up)

♥

Uno (International Games) is a great game to play. The hours fly by.

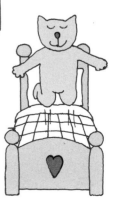

CARDS

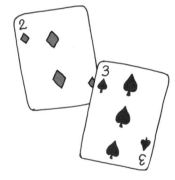

SPIT

You will need a standard deck of cards. The object is to get rid of all of your cards. "Spit" requires quick thinking and the ability to make on-the-spot decisions. You also need to be pretty fast with your fingers, because some quick movement by one player can overwhelm his opponent.

The two players sit facing each other. One shuffles the deck and divides it evenly between them, forming two face-down stacks. Holding his own pile face down in one hand, each player deals out four of his own cards side by side face up in front of him. The four cards are called his "spread." The game is played without turns, each opponent playing simultaneously, and as quickly as possible. To start the game, both players count "One, two, three . . . *Spit!*" and slap one card each face up in the center of the table between them. These cards start the two center piles.

Now each player goes into action instantly, trying to rid himself of cards by slapping cards from his spread onto the top card of either of the growing center piles. A card can be placed on a center pile if it is either one above or one below the pile's top card (for example, if you start with a five, the next card could be a six, then a seven, then a six, then a five). When an empty spot is left open in a player's spread, he can fill it with a card from his stock. Cards of the same rank appearing in his spread can be placed on top of one another, leaving space for more cards from the stock. Spread cards that have been doubled up may only be taken off one at a time to place on center piles.

When no more plays are possible, the players stop and Spit once more, throwing two more cards down on top of the center piles. If this happens when one player has exhausted all the cards in his stock but still has one or more cards left in his spread, only the player still holding cards in his stock Spits. When one player has exhausted all the cards in both his stock and spread, he cries, "Stop!" and the round ends. The player without cards then selects the smaller of the two center piles to form his new stock, and his opponent gets the larger pile.

The players shuffle their stocks, deal their spreads, and the game resumes with a Spit. Since having the greater number of cards is a disadvantage, the player losing the first round has an increased chance of losing the second, and an even greater chance of losing the third. Eventually, the game will reach a point where one player will be without cards in his stock after dealing out his spread at the beginning of a round. When this happens, that player is the winner.

(Ages 8 and up)

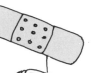

CARDS

When Ruth Bloom's kids were sick she would play finger games on their backs so they would relax. She would spell words on their backs or draw simple shapes and they would have to concentrate and figure out what she had traced with her finger.

GO FISH

The object of this card game is to collect the most sets of four matching cards, or to be the first to get rid of all the cards in your hand. The dealer deals out five cards to himself and to each of the other players. He places the rest of the deck face down in the center. Starting with the dealer, each player in turn calls out the name of any other player and asks that player to hand over cards he needs. For example, if a player has a three in his hand, on his turn he might ask another player, "Sarah, give me all of your threes." If Sarah has any threes, she has to hand them all over. If Sarah doesn't have any threes, she says, "Go Fish!" and the player who asked must pick a card from the pile in the center.

A player can repeat his turn over and over as long as he gets the cards he wants from another player or the Go Fish pile. When he fails to draw the card he wants, he loses his turn and another player goes. Four matching cards of the same rank (such as four 3's or four jacks) make a "book." Whenever a player gets a book of cards, he immediately takes those cards out of his hand and puts them face up in front of him.

The Gilbars and the Brokaws disagree on how you finally win at "Go Fish." In the Gilbars' version, the game ends when there are no more cards in the Go Fish pile. Each player then counts his books and the one with the most books wins. During the time the Brokaw girls were playing this game, the first person to get rid of all the cards in his hand was the winner.

(Ages 4 and up)

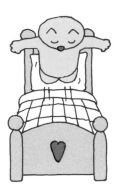

OLD MAID

You will need an Old Maid deck or a standard deck of fifty-two cards from which three queens have been removed.

The object is to gather pairs and put down all the cards in your hand, without getting stuck with the "Old Maid" (the queen). Deal out all the cards (it doesn't matter if the cards don't divide evenly).

After the cards have been dealt, the players look at their hands and place any pairs they may have face up in front of them. When all the players have removed the pairs from their hands, they take turns pulling one card from the hand of the player to their right (without peeking, of course!). If a player draws a match to one of the cards in his hand, he adds the pair to those already in front of him.

When all the cards have been paired up and discarded, the player left with the unmatched queen or Old Maid card is the loser. A hint from Gabe Gordon: It is bad luck to get stuck with the Old Maid, so try to make sure another player gets the bad luck by making the card stick out or look especially inviting and tempting him to draw it. When Gabe's sister, Mandy, figured this out, she faked him out by tempting Gabe with other cards, pretending that they were the Old Maid.

(Ages 4 and up)

WAR

This is Lisa Gilbar's favorite card game because it goes on forever. Annie has been known to win (she says twice, Lisa says maybe once). It's a great game to play when a child is sick because it doesn't take a lot of thinking—the card just has to have the higher number to win a round.

Divide the deck in two, so that each player has twenty-six cards. Each player puts his cards face down in a neat pile in front of him so no one can see them. Then both players simultaneously turn up one card each and place them side by side in the center of the playing surface. The player with the higher card keeps both and puts them underneath his stack. (In "War" the ace is the highest card.) When both cards are the same number (or, as Lisa says, in the same "battalion"), a "war" commences. Each player yells "war" and then places three cards, face down, on the "war" card. Then they both turn the fourth card face up and the one with the higher number wins all the cards (that will be ten cards). If, by chance, the final "war" cards also match, you have another war.

(Ages 6 and up)

CARDS

THE WINNER

SAMPLE WAR

Wesley Schwartz broke his leg and had to have a cast all the way up to his thigh. In the beginning it hurt so badly he couldn't sleep, so his parents had middle-of-the-night entertainment all lined up. Sometimes they played cards or watched videos, depending on how tired everyone was.

PENNY BASEBALL

You will need one die and at least two players. Draw a baseball diamond on a piece of paper, putting in the three bases and home plate. Use three pennies for men. Throw the die to start the game—the player with the highest number is at bat.

"Penny Baseball" is played like the real game. While you are at bat, a throw of one, two, or three stands for a single, double, or triple, respectively. When you make hits, advance your penny men around the paper diamond to correspond to a real baseball game. Every time a man reaches home base, you score a run. A roll of four is a home run, and all the men already on the diamond score as well as the hitter. If you roll a six, your batter has struck out. If you roll a five, it's as if your batter hit the ball and it was successfully fielded and thrown, giving the other team a possible double play. Not only is the man at bat out, the men on base may also be out as follows:

★ If only one man is on base, he is out.
★ If you have men on first and second base, the man on second is out.
★ If you have men on second and third base, they are both safe.
★ If you have men on all bases, only the man on first is out. When a man is out, remove him from the diamond. After three outs, your inning ends and you pass the die to your opponent. After you have each played nine innings, the one who scored the most runs is the winner.

(Ages 6 and up)

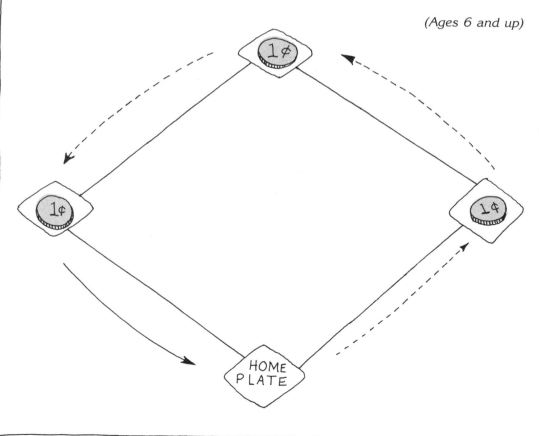

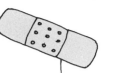

PORCUPINE

You will need one die for this game. The object of "Porcupine" is to be the first player to complete the drawing of a porcupine. The porcupine has thirteen parts: the body, the head, the tail, two eyes, two feet, and six needles. Each part of the porcupine has a different number value: 1 point for the body, 2 points for the head, 3 points for each needle, 4 points for each eye, 5 points for each foot, and 6 points for the tail. To complete the whole porcupine, you must throw a 1, a 2, six 3s, two 4s, two 5s, and a 6.

Each player throws the die only once in each round. Before a player can start drawing his porcupine he must throw a 1. Only then can he draw the body. Once the body is drawn, he may start adding the head, feet, and tail when he throws the appropriate numbers with the die. The eyes, however, cannot be added until after he has thrown a 2, because he has to draw the head onto the body before he can add the eyes.

(Ages 5 and up)

ONE DIE

PAPER

PENCIL

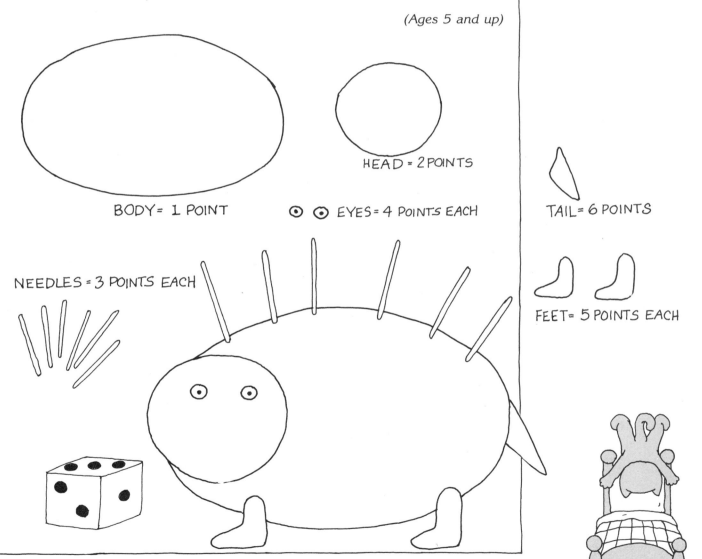

BODY = 1 POINT

HEAD = 2 POINTS

⊙ ⊙ EYES = 4 POINTS EACH

TAIL = 6 POINTS

NEEDLES = 3 POINTS EACH

FEET = 5 POINTS EACH

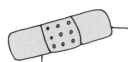

106

3 DICE

THE ROLL OF THE DICE

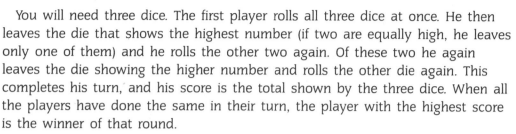

You will need three dice. The first player rolls all three dice at once. He then leaves the die that shows the highest number (if two are equally high, he leaves only one of them) and he rolls the other two again. Of these two he again leaves the die showing the higher number and rolls the other die again. This completes his turn, and his score is the total shown by the three dice. When all the players have done the same in their turn, the player with the highest score is the winner of that round.

You play as many rounds as you want. When the game is over, the player who has won the most rounds is the winner.

(Ages 7 and up)

TWENTY-ONE

Two or more can play the famous casino game of blackjack or "Twenty-one." For our version, you won't even need a deck of cards. The only requirement is that the players know how to add (it's a great teaching game!). You will need pennies, buttons, or poker chips and dice.

Each player puts one penny into the pot. Each player in turn then rolls the dice as many times as he likes, adding up the numbers thrown, in an attempt to get a total of twenty-one or as near as possible to it. A player whose total goes over twenty-one is out of the game. Whoever has a total closest to twenty-one gets the pot.

(Ages 5 and up)

2 DICE

BUTTONS, PENNIES, OR POKER CHIPS

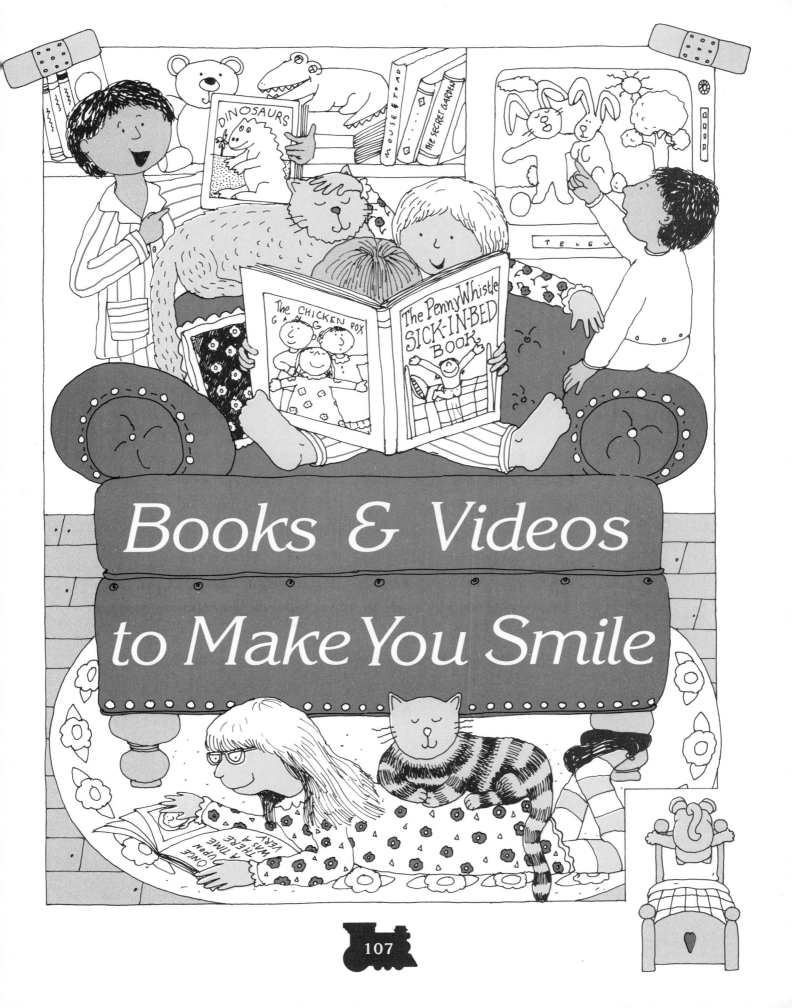

Books & Videos
to Make You Smile

♥

Judy Shunk, the librarian at the Northern Middle School in Dillsburg, PA, polled her students and discovered that most of them like to be read to when they are sick as opposed to reading by themselves (even the twelve- and thirteen-year-olds).

Aside from games, activities, projects, and yes, even some television, books and videos are fabulous ways to transport your child to another world. Books still remain the most wonderful, magical entertainment for children. When your child is in the beginning of his illness he may not feel well enough to read to himself. This is the perfect time for you to read to your child. Although the classics always work, we have found that humor and laughter are truly the best medicine. With that thought in mind we have put together the following section, which we call "Books and Videos to Make You Smile."

The lists of books are arranged by age, but these are subjective compilations. You know your child best. If your child is more sophisticated than other four-year-olds, a book that is listed for an older child might be more appropriate. Conversely, a child of eight who normally reads at the level of a ten-year-old, may, when he is ill, prefer to read a book that would be too easy for him at other times. Thus, as always, you and your child together are the best judges of what books to choose.

Videos can capture children's imaginations and allow their minds to travel to faraway lands. When your child is not feeling well, or is bedridden, videos are the perfect diversion. Just pop his favorite videotape, or one of the many we have listed here, into your video player and your child will be occupied, entertained, and laughing for hours!

Our video list includes viewing choices for children of different ages and with different interests. We have included musicals, animated cartoons, science-fiction odysseys, and many adventures. You and your child will know best which videos are, in terms of age and subject matter, appropriate for his viewing.

BOOKS

GETTING BETTER BOOKS

This collection of books includes stories of children who are sick in bed, in the hospital, and dealing with fears of their illnesses. Shared experiences always bring the greatest of comfort and books can be the perfect friend.

Anna's Special Present, by Yoriko Tsutsui. London: Viking Kestrel, 1988.
When Anna's little sister Katy suddenly goes to the hospital, Anna knows exactly what gift to bring her.

The Best Cat Suit of All, by Sylvia Cassedy. New York: Dial Books for Young Readers, 1991.
Mike is sick in bed on Halloween and can't wear his cat suit. None of his visitors can cheer him up until someone arrives wearing the best cat suit ever.

Betsy and the Doctor, by Gunilla Wolde. New York: Random House, 1977.
Betsy falls from a tree, hits her head, and must visit the hospital emergency room to see a doctor.

Carousel, by Brian Wildsmith. New York: Knopf, 1988.
A little girl dreams of riding on her favorite merry-go-round while sick in bed.

Crocodile Plaster, by Marjorie-Ann Watts. London: A. Deutsch, 1978.
Julie's boring day in the hospital is suddenly brightened when a crocodile is admitted with broken legs.

Curious George Goes to the Hospital, by Margret and H.A. Rey, in collaboration with the Children's Hospital Medical Center, Boston. Boston: Houghton Mifflin Company, 1966.
After swallowing a piece of his jigsaw puzzle, Curious George goes to the hospital.

Elizabeth Gets Well, by Alfons Weber, M.D. New York: Thomas Y. Crowell, 1970.
Elizabeth learns about the hospital when she is admitted to have her appendix removed.

Emergency Mouse, by Bernard Stone. Englewood Cliffs: Prentice-Hall, 1978.
Henry, in the hospital for an operation, discovers that a group of mice operate a hospital of their own in the wall of his room.

Eric Needs Stitches, by Barbara Pavis Marino. Reading, Mass.: Addison-Wesley, 1979.
Eric is afraid because he must go to the hospital emergency room to get stitches in his knee after a bad fall.

♥

Joan Talarico and her son, Nicholas, who was frequently home for that initial day of an ear infection before the antibiotics worked their magic, would stop at the library on their way home from the doctor and pharmacy. They would then choose books long enough to be read in several sittings. This left something to look forward to throughout the day.

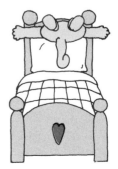

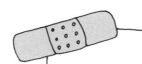

Feel Better, Ernest!, by Gabrielle Vincent. New York: Greenwillow, 1988.

Celestine, a mouse, takes very good care of Ernest, a bear, while he is sick.

Henry and Mudge Get the Cold Shivers: The Seventh Book of Their Adventures, by Cynthia Rylant. New York: Bradbury Press, 1989.

Mudge gets sick unexpectedly and Henry does all that he can to make her feel better.

I Wish I Was Sick, Too!, by Franz Brandenberg. New York: Greenwillow, 1976.

Elizabeth is envious of all the attention her brother receives when he is sick in bed—and then she gets sick.

If You Want to Scare Yourself, by Angela Sommer-Bodenburg. New York: Lippincott, 1989.

Bored and sick in bed, Freddy listens to his family members tell scary stories and then makes one up himself.

Island Rescue, by Charles E. Martin. New York: Greenwillow, 1985.

Mae breaks her leg and must be taken by boat off the island where she lives to the hospital on the mainland.

Morris Has a Cold, written and illustrated by Bernard Wiseman. New York: Dodd, Mead, 1978.

Morris, a moose, has a cold so Borris, a bear, tries to cure him.

No Mail for Mitchell, by Catherine Siracusa. New York: Random House, 1990.

Mitchell, a mailman, delivers mail to all the animals but never receives any mail himself until he is sick for a day.

The Old Witch and Her Magic Basket, by Ida DeLage. Champaign, Ill.: Garrard Publishing Company, 1978.

An old witch entertains a little girl who is sick on Halloween.

One Bear in the Hospital, by Caroline Bucknall. New York: Dial Books for Young Readers, 1991.

Ted Bear breaks his leg and stays overnight in the hospital.

One Day, Two Dragons, by Lynne Bertrand. New York: Clarkson Potter, 1992.

Tells the story of one day when two dragons go to 3 Bug Street for a doctor's appointment and receive four vaccinations! Find out what happens in this book and learn that a doctor's visit can be very funny.

Poor Monty, by Anne Fine. New York: Clarion Books, 1991.

Monty isn't feeling well and needs his mom, who is a doctor, to take care of him.

Sick in Bed, by Anne and Harlow Rockwell. New York: Macmillan, 1982.

A little boy with a sore throat describes his feelings and experiences.

♥

Throughout his nearly year-long recuperation, Jeff Buhai's main goal was to become an expert in things he didn't know before. For example, he set himself a goal to study one country at a time and become an expert in that country. He also picked a favorite author and read everything he could by that author. This made him feel more important than all the other kids who were going to school because in this way he was able to learn things at his own pace and to a degree that made him feel smarter and more accomplished than the kids that were well.

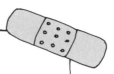

The Sick-in-Bed Birthday, by Linda Wagner Tyler. New York: Viking Kestrel, 1988.
  The school nurse sends Tucky Pig home from school on the day of his birthday party and he's convinced it will be the worst birthday ever.

Someday with My Father, by Helen Elizabeth Buckley. New York: Harper & Row, 1985.
  A little girl imagines the fun she will have with her father when her broken leg heals.

Spot Visits the Hospital, by Eric Hill. New York: G.P. Putnam's Sons, 1987.
  Spot, a dog, explores the hospital during a visit to his friend Steve.

Tales for a Winter's Eve, by Wendy Watson. New York: Farrar, Straus & Giroux, 1988.
  Freddie Fox injures his paw in a skiing accident and his family and friends distract him with stories about animals who live in their village.

Teddy Bears Cure a Cold, by Susanna Gretz and Alison Sage. New York: Four Winds Press, 1984.
  William has had a cold for so long the teddy bears decide to work their own cure.

This Little Nose, by Jan Ormerod. New York: Lothrop, Lee & Shepard Books, 1987.
  Baby gets a nose cold so Mom cheers him up by showing him noses on a doll, a cat, and a teddy bear.

Tomato Soup, by Thacher Hurd. New York: Crown Publishers, 1992.
  Baby Mouse catches a cold and finds a way to avoid taking her medicine.

Toot!, by Taro Gomi. New York: William Morrow, 1979.
  Albert's trumpet has the flu and he knows just what to do.

What the Mailman Brought, by Carolyn Craven. New York: G.P. Putnam's Sons, 1987.
  William is sick, can't go to school, and a mysterious mailman delivers unusual packages every day.

When Francie Was Sick, by Holly Keller. New York: Greenwillow, 1985.
  Mama takes care of Francie when she is sick at home.

Who's Sick Today?, by Lynne Cherry. New York: Dutton, 1988.
  The reader is introduced to a variety of animals with different illnesses.

The Winter Day, by Beverly Komoda. New York: HarperCollins, 1991.
  The rabbit children build the biggest snow rabbit in the world, making sure it is tall enough to be seen by their brother who is inside with a bad cold.

BOOKS TO MAKE YOU SMILE

Under Five

Bedtime for Frances, by Russell Hoban. New York: Harper & Row, 1960.
Frances does not want to go to bed. Read and discover what happens before she finally falls asleep.

Before I Go to Sleep, written by Thomas Hood, illustrated by Maryjane Begin-Callanan. New York: G. P. Putnam's Sons, 1990.
Instead of sleeping, a boy imagines all the animals he would like to be.

Bunny Surprise, by Lena Anderson. New York: R&S Books, 1986.
Bunny helps a little boy find his pacifier among familiar fruits and vegetables in this picture book.

Bye-Bye, Baby: A Sad Story with a Happy Ending, by Janet and Allan Ahlberg. Boston: Little, Brown, 1989.
A baby who lives all by himself goes in search of a mommy and daddy and friends.

Chicken Soup with Rice: A Book of Months, by Maurice Sendak. New York: Harper & Row, 1962.
"Each month is gay, each season nice, when eating chicken soup with rice."

Color Farm, by Lois Ehlert. New York: Lippincott, 1990.
Animals on a farm are made up of colorful shapes. Ehlert is also the author of *Color Zoo* (New York: Lippincott, 1989).

Daddy Makes the Best Spaghetti, by Anna Grossnickle Hines. New York: Clarion Books, 1986.
Corey's father makes the best spaghetti and does a lot of neat tricks.

Frog and Toad Are Friends, by Arnold Lobel. New York: Harper & Row, 1970.
Frog and Toad are best friends. Read about their adventures in *Frog and Toad Together* (New York: Harper & Row, 1972), *Frog and Toad All Year* (New York: Harper & Row, 1976), and *Days with Frog and Toad* (New York: Harper & Row, 1979), as well.

I'm a Little Mouse: A Touch and Feel Book, by Noelle and David Carter. New York: Henry Holt, 1990.
A little mouse meets a variety of animals who describe their differences. The illustrations have textured patches that simulate the coats of the animals.

♥

Christie Mitchell reads four-year-old Morgan's favorite stories on tape so that Morgan can play them back when her mother can't be with her.

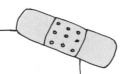

***The Jolly Postman* or *Other People's Letters*,** by Janet and Allan Ahlberg. Boston: Little, Brown, 1986.

The Jolly Postman delivers mail to favorite fairy-tale characters. Cards and letters are included and may be removed and read.

***King Bidgood's in the Bathtub*,** written by Audrey Wood and illustrated by Don Wood. San Diego: Harcourt Brace Jovanovich, 1985.

King Bidgood will not get out of the bathtub to rule his kingdom. How do his subjects ever get him out? Great illustrations.

***Madeline*,** by Ludwig Bemelmans. New York: The Viking Press, 1967.

"In an old house in Paris that was covered with vines lived twelve little girls in two straight lines."

***Now We Are Six*,** by A. A. Milne. New York: Dutton, 1961.

Another classic from the author of *Winnie-the-Pooh*. Includes the poem about "sneezles and wheezles."

***Sloppy Kisses*,** by Elizabeth Winthrop. New York: Macmillan, 1980.

Emmy Lou's friend informs her that kissing is for babies—so she tries to make do with a pat on the shoulder.

***The Snowy Day*,** by Jack Ezra Keats. New York: Viking Press, 1962.

Peter spends a day in the city playing in the snow.

***Sophie and Lou*,** by Petra Mathers. New York: HarperCollins, 1991.

When shy Sophie's interest is piqued by the sight of people dancing in the studio across the street, she sets out to learn to dance on her own.

***The Three Little Pigs*,** retold and illustrated by James Marshall. New York: Dial Books for Young Readers, 1989.

This classic tale is retold with exciting illustrations.

***The Very Hungry Caterpillar*,** by Eric Carle. New York: Philomel Books, 1979.

Follow this caterpillar as he eats his way through different foods and discover where he ends up.

***The Wheels on the Bus*,** adapted and illustrated by Paul O. Zelinsky. New York: Dutton's Children's Books, 1990.

A favorite lyric is turned into a pop-up picture book filled with fun characters and parts that move.

***Where the Wild Things Are*,** by Maurice Sendak. New York: Harper & Row, 1963.

A naughty boy, sent to bed without supper, sails away to an island inhabited by monsters and is made king, only to find it was all a dream.

Five to Ten

Aesop's Fables, compiled by Russell Ash and Bernard Higton. San Francisco: Chronicle Books, 1990.

An illustrated version of this childhood classic is full of the best-known fables: "The Hare and the Tortoise," "The Boy Who Cried Wolf," "The Lion and the Mouse," and many more.

Aida, told by Leontyne Price, illustrated by Leo and Diane Dillon. San Diego: Gulliver/Harcourt Brace Jovanovich, 1990.

Verdi's famous tragedy *Aida* is told here by the opera diva famed for her portrayal of the enslaved Ethiopian princess who falls in love with the Egyptian general.

Amelia Bedelia, by Peggy Parish. New York: Harper & Row, 1963.

Amelia Bedelia, Mr. and Mrs. Rogers' new maid, does *exactly* as they tell her—with disastrous and amusing results. Look for other Amelia Bedelia stories.

Animalia, by Graeme Base. New York: Harry N. Abrams, 1986.

Each page of this alphabet book is comprised of stunning images of animals all starting with the letter on that page.

Basil of Baker Street, by Eve Titus. New York: Whittlesly House, 1958.

The tale of a mouse detective and his adventures while solving a case. *Basil in Mexico* (New York: Simon & Schuster, 1976) and *Basil in the Wild West* (New York: McGraw-Hill, 1982) are other great books.

Beach Ball, by Peter Sis. New York: Greenwillow, 1990.

Mary and her mom take a trip to the beach. Readers are directed (by clever clues) to hunt for letters, numbers, animals, opposites, colors, and shapes.

The Big Book for Peace, edited by Ann Durell and Marilyn Sachs. New York: Dutton's Children's Books, 1990.

This book, created by over thirty of the best-known children's authors and illustrators, is filled with stories, pictures, songs, and poems of peace.

Catch That Cat!: A Picture Book of Rhymes and Puzzles, written and illustrated by Monika Beisner. New York: Farrar, Straus and Giroux, 1990.

Sixteen picture puzzles about cats. Poems give instructions on how to solve the puzzles.

Charlie and the Chocolate Factory, by Roald Dahl. New York: Knopf, 1964.

Willy Wonka's contest allows five lucky winners to visit his chocolate factory. Discover who wins and what adventures await them. Also read Dahl's classic *James and the Giant Peach* (New York: Knopf, 1961).

Charlotte's Web, by E. B. White. New York: Harper & Row, 1952.

Fern lives on a farm with Wilbur (a pig), Templeton (a rat), and Charlotte (a spider), who saves Wilbur's life.

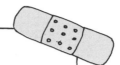

Cricket in Times Square, by George Selden. New York: Farrar, Straus & Giroux, 1960.

Read about a special cricket found by Mario and his mouse Tucker in Times Square.

The Eleventh Hour: A Curious Mystery, by Graeme Base. New York: Harry N. Abrams, 1989.

When Horace the Elephant turns eleven he invites all of his friends to a birthday party. But when it's time to eat, Horace and his guests realize the birthday feast is gone. The reader tries to catch the thief.

The Furry News: How to Make a Newspaper, written and illustrated by Loreen Leedy. New York: Holiday House, 1990.

Everything kids need to know to start their own family, neighborhood, or school newspaper.

Gorilla/Chinchilla, by Bert Kitchen. New York: Dial Books, 1990.

Kitchen's original and witty verse centers on pairs of animals.

Kay Thompson's Eloise: A Book for Precocious Grown Ups, by Kay Thompson. New York: Simon & Schuster, 1983.

Eloise is a mischievous little girl who lives in the Plaza Hotel in New York City. Your child can experience a day in the life of Eloise and join in her adventures.

The Knight and the Dragon, by Tomie de Paola. New York: G.P. Putnam's Sons, 1980.

An inexperienced knight and a dragon prepare to meet in their first battle.

Look!: The Ultimate Spot-the-Difference Book, illustrated by April Wilson, with nature notes by A. J. Wood. New York: Dial Books for Young Readers, 1990.

Each spread shows what appears to be two identical scenes—but appearances can be deceiving.

The Mouse and the Motorcycle, by Beverly Cleary. New York: William Morrow, 1965.

Ralph, a mouse, meets Keith, a boy, who has a motorcycle just his size. Learn of their adventures and special friendship.

Mr. Popper's Penguins, by Richard and Florence Atwater. Boston: Little, Brown, 1938.

Twelve penguins become part of the Popper family. Mr. Popper forms a plan to pay for all of their expenses—the penguins will be vaudeville performers!

Nate the Great, by Marjorie Weiman Sharmat. New York: Coward, McCann & Geoghegan, 1972.

Nate the Great is a detective who solves many mysteries. This time he must find Annie's dog Fang. Sharmat has written other Nate the Great stories—check for them in your library.

Pippi Longstocking, by Astrid Lindgren. New York: Viking Press, 1950.

Pippi lives in a house at the edge of a Swedish village with a monkey, a horse, and no parents.

Ten and Up

Freckle Juice, by Judy Blume. New York: Four Winds Press, 1971.

Andrew wants freckles so much that he buys Sharon's freckle recipe for fifty cents.

From the Mixed-up Files of Mrs. Basil E. Frankweiler, by E. L. Konigsburg. New York: Atheneum, 1967.

In order to teach her parents a lesson, Claudia decides to run away—to the Metropolitan Museum of Art—and invites her brother to go with her. Read and learn why Claudia doesn't want to leave the museum.

Henry in Shadowland, by Laszlo Varvasovszky. Boston: D. R. Godine, 1990.

Henry and his big friend Paul make a shadow box with cutouts of a dragon and other characters. Preparing for the big performance, Henry becomes part of the action.

The Lion, the Witch and the Wardrobe, by C.S. Lewis. New York: Macmillan, 1950.

Four children enter the magical world of Narnia through the back of a wardrobe where they meet Aslan, the golden lion, and the white witch. Read *Prince Caspian: The Return to Narnia* (New York: Macmillan, 1951) and the other books of *The Chronicles of Narnia.*

Little House on the Prairie, by Laura Ingalls Wilder. New York: Harper, 1953.

Laura Ingalls Wilder tells the story of her own experience when her family moved from the Wisconsin woods to the prairie. Wilder has written many stories about her life on the prairie including *Long Winter* (New York: Harper, 1953), *On the Banks of Plum Creek* (New York: Harper, 1953), and *Farmer Boy* (New York: Harper, 1953), as well as many other classics.

Sarah, Plain and Tall, by Patricia McLachlan. New York: Harper & Row, 1985.

Sarah answers an ad to be a mail-order bride placed by a man living in Kansas with two children, Caleb and Anna. Read about Sarah's adventures moving from Maine and living in Kansas with her new family.

The Secret Garden, by Frances Hodgson Burnett. Philadelphia: Lippincott, 1962.

A turn-of-the-century masterpiece about a little orphan girl who comes to live in a big house in the north of England. She soon discovers the magic that lies in the secret garden.

Shoebag, by Mary James. New York: Scholastic, Inc., 1990.

A twist on Kafka's "Metamorphosis," a young cockroach awakes to find that he has been turned into a human boy. Find out what happens after he is adopted by the Biddle family.

Soup, by Robert Newton Peck. New York: Knopf, 1974.

Soup and Rob are best friends, living in a small Vermont town, who find amusement and fun. *Soup and Me* (New York: Knopf, 1975) follows their continuing adventures and antics.

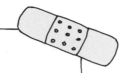

Superfudge and ***Fudge-a-Mania,*** by Judy Blume. New York: Dutton's Children's Books, 1980 and 1990, respectively.

In both books, the antics and adventures of Peter and his little brother, Fudge, are brought to life.

This Place Has No Atmosphere, by Paula Danziger. New York: Delacorte, 1986.

It is the twenty-first century and Aurora loves living on planet Earth. However, she soon learns that her family is moving to the moon!

Where the Sidewalk Ends, by Shel Silverstein. New York: Harper & Row, 1974.

A collection of poems and drawings by Silverstein that will make everyone giggle. *A Light in the Attic* (New York: Harper & Row, 1981) is another favorite.

BOOKS ON TAPE

FAIRY TALES

Beauty and the Beast. Read by Bess Armstrong. Dove Kids/Dove Audio. Call (800) 328-DOVE or (800) 345-9945 inside California.

Bess Armstrong shares this fairy tale in which a merchant's daughter sacrifices herself to a "beast" to save her father.

The Chronicles of Narnia, by C.S. Lewis. Caedmon.

All seven stories that comprise *The Chronicles of Narnia* are available on Caedmon recordings. Each story is read by a different actor including Ian Richardson.

"Cinderella" and ***"Yeh-Shen,"*** by The Brothers Grimm and Ai-Ling Louie, respectively. Read by Joan Chen. Dove Kids/Dove Audio. Call (800) 328-DOVE or (800) 345-9945 inside California.

Side one tells the story of "Cinderella" and side two tells the original Chinese version, which many people believe was the basis for The Brothers Grimm tale.

Curious George Learns the Alphabet and Other Stories About Curious George, by Margaret and H.A. Rey. Read by Julie Harris. Caedmon.

Listen to the tales of a favorite monkey including *Curious George Flies a Kite* and *Curious George Goes to the Hospital.*

Day at the Zoo and ***Day at the Aquarium***. Read by Mary Sheldon. Dove Kids/Dove Audio. Call (800) 328-DOVE or (800) 345-9945 inside California.

Each of these "Learn and Draw Audios" comes with a thirty-minute tape, a poster to color, and colored pencils. The tapes introduce children to animal sounds and gives them the opportunity to act out parts along with the story characters.

♥

Joan Talarico had audio books on hand when her kids were sick. This freed her time and occupied a child too sick to even watch television.

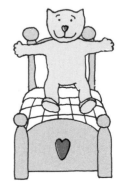

"The Emperor's New Clothes" and *"The Ugly Duckling,"* by Hans Christian Andersen. Read by Michael York. Dove Kids/Dove Audio. Call (800) 328-DOVE or (800) 345-9945 inside California.

These two tales illustrate the point that appearances can be deceiving. Humorous and engaging.

The Great Brain, by John D. Fitzgerald. Performed by Morgan White. The Great Brain Enterprise.

Ten-year-old Tom D. Fitzgerald is "The Great Brain." Listen to eight stories including: *The Great Brain Saves the Day* and *The Magic Water Closet.*

The Happy Prince, by Oscar Wilde. Read by Dudley Moore. Dove Kids/Dove Audio. Call (800) 328-DOVE or (800) 345-9945 inside California.

This is the classic story of a prince who values love and loyalty over gold.

Keepers of the Animals: Native American Animal Stories from *Keepers of the Animals* by Michael J. Caduto and Joseph Bruchac. Told by Joseph Bruchac. Fulcrum Publishing, (800) 992-2908.

Twenty-four traditional tales about the powers of animals.

The Moon Lady, adapted by Amy Tan from her book, *The Joy Luck Club.* Read by Amy Tan. Dove Kids/Dove Audio. Call (800) 328-DOVE or (800) 345-9945 inside California.

A grandmother tells her grandchildren the tale of the Moon Lady who appears on the evening of the Moon Festival and grants secret wishes.

The Phantom Tollbooth, by Norton Juster. Performed by Pat Carroll. Caedmon.

Milo is bored until he arrives home from school to find a strange cardboard box complete with a tollbooth and maps and his fantastic adventures begin.

The Prince and the Pauper, by Mark Twain. Read by Ian Richardson. Caedmon.

Listen to this timeless classic about two boys who are almost exactly alike and decide to switch identities and lives.

"Rumpelstiltskin" and *"Rapunzel,"* by The Brothers Grimm. Read by Dudley Moore. Dove Kids/Dove Audio. Call (800) 328-DOVE or (800) 345-9945 inside California.

In "Rumpelstiltskin," a mysterious man shows a girl how to turn straw into gold. "Rapunzel" is the tale of a princess who is trapped in a tower by a sorceress. When a prince falls in love with her he must find a way to rescue the princess.

Story of the Nutcracker, by E.T.A. Hoffman. Adapted by Janet Schulman. Read by Claire Bloom. Caedmon.

This recording combines an adaptation of Hoffman's original story with music by Tchaikovsky.

The Story of Peter Pan, by J.M. Barrie. Read by Glynis Johns. Caedmon.

Learn of the adventures of the Darling children, Nana, and Peter Pan as they are performed in a lively fashion.

The Velveteen Rabbit, by Margery Williams. Read by Gwen Verdon. Caedmon.
What makes this velveteen rabbit "real"? Listen and find out.

Winnie-the-Pooh and Eeyore, by A.A. Milne. Told and sung by Carol Channing.
Caedmon.
Carole Channing brings this story about a modest bear and a gloomy
donkey to life.

VIDEOS

Order the videos listed below through video stores or mail-order firms such as
Music for Little People, (800) 346-4445. Also, check your local library—you may
find them on loan.

American Storytelling Series. H. W. Wilson Co., (800) 367-6770.
Some of the best professional storytellers, such as Jay O'Callahan, David Holt,
and Diane Wolkstein, delve into mythology, folklore, and real life, spinning tales
from around the globe.

An American Tail. MCA Home Video.
This animated adventure features Fievel, a young mouse separated from his
family in scary New York City at the turn of the century. (Rated G, but it might
be frightening for younger viewers.)

Baby Songs Presents John Lithgow's Kid-Size Concert. Hi-Tops Video.
John Lithgow sings funny songs while accompanying himself on the guitar.

Beauty and the Beast. Hi-Tops Video.
Using different voices, Mia Farrow tells the tale of Beauty, the merchant's
beautiful daughter, who is condemned to live with a hideous yet kindly beast in
his castle.

The Cat in the Hat Comes Back. Random House Home Video.
Dr. Seuss's drawings are part of the attraction in this story in which the mischievous title character returns to Sally and her brother's house to wreak more
havoc while their mother is away. Two other Dr. Seuss books also appear on
this video: *There's a Wocket in My Pocket!* and *Fox in Socks*.

Chitty Chitty Bang Bang. CBS/Fox.
The classic story of a daydreaming inventor and his car that does magical
things.

David Holt, Storyteller: The Hogaphone and Other Stories. High Windy Video, (800) 63-STORY.

A telephone made of groundhog hides and wire, a dancing bear, a man-eating witch, magic corn, and three brave dogs—Holt inspires laughs as he draws on southern tales and folklore.

Dinosaurs, Dinosaurs, Dinosaurs. Twin Tower Enterprises, Inc. Distributed by Prime Cuts.

Each tape comes with an inflatable dinosaur to increase dinomania.

Dr. Seuss's ABC. Random House Home Video.

Dr. Seuss makes up words to go with letters, and his illustrations will make your child laugh.

E.T. The Extra-Terrestrial. MCA Home Video.

An extraterrestrial is stranded on earth and befriended by a little boy and his family.

Fun in a Box. Made-to-Order Productions, (800) 232-5252.

This is an eclectic series of award-winning animation and live-action shorts for all ages. It includes Chris Van Allsburg's *Ben's Dreams*, the strikingly animated *Metal Dogs of India*, and a quirky film called *Fish*, about three Keats-quoting detectives.

Good Morning, Good Night. Bo Peep Productions, P. O. Box 982, Eureka, MT 59917, or call (406) 889-3225.

From the rooster's crow at daybreak, a young farm boy and the farm animals go about their daily routines.

History Rock, Grammar Rock, Science Rock, and ***Multiplication Rock.*** Golden Book Video.

School House Rock, the classic series of animated educational shorts that ran between Saturday morning cartoons on ABC, is being released on four tapes.

The Jungle Book. Walt Disney Home Video.

This is Disney's animated classic based on Rudyard Kipling's *Jungle Book*, in which Mowgli is raised in the jungle with wolves and other animals.

Kids in Motion. Fox Video.

Scott Baio hosts this video that encourages children to work on their strength and coordination using dance, poetry, and songs by The Temptations.

Labyrinth. Nelson Entertainment.

A teenage girl's baby brother is kidnapped by goblins and she is forced to enter a magical labyrinth to find him. She is helped by Jim Henson's strange creatures.

Looney Tunes. Warner Home Video.

These cartoons and compilations will keep your child thoroughly entertained.

The Love Bug. Walt Disney Home Video.

Herbie, a Volkswagen Bug, has human feelings and magical powers. In this film, Herbie helps a race car driver win a road race by fighting a villain.

Lyle, Lyle, Crocodile. Hi-Tops Video / Video Treasures.

With a score by Charles Strouse, narration by Tony Randall, this unusual story about a beloved crocodile is a family treat.

Mary Poppins. Walt Disney Home Video.

Julie Andrews is the world's greatest nanny, Mary Poppins. She and Uncle Bert, the chimney sweep, take the Banks children on fantastic adventures.

The Maurice Sendak Library. Children's Circle Home Video.

This is an anthology of illustrated stories. *Alligators All Around*, an alphabet poem, *Pierre* (about a boy who simply doesn't care about anything), and *Chicken Soup with Rice* are accompanied by original music composed and sung by Carole King. *Where the Wild Things Are* is a semianimated version of the story of Max, a child named "King of the Wild Things" by the Wild Things themselves. *In the Night Kitchen* tells the story of Mickey and how he supplied milk to three bakers so that everyone could have bread in the morning.

Monster Hits! Random House Home Video.

This is an all-monster, all-music extravaganza with the Muppets.

The Mouse and the Motorcycle. ABC Kidtime Home Video from Strand VCI Entertainment, (800) 922-3827.

This award-winning film, based on Beverly Cleary's book about the friendship between a hot-rodding mouse named Ralph and a lonely boy, is a zany combination of live-action and stop-motion animation.

The Muppet Movie. CBS/Fox Video.

Kermit the Frog hits Hollywood to break into show business and finds himself being chased by Doc Hopper, who wants him to be a "spokesfrog" for a fried-frog's-leg chain. Miss Piggy and the rest of the Muppets join in the fun.

The Muppets Take Manhattan. CBS/Fox Video.

The Muppets have a big hit with a college variety show. They decide to take the show on the road—heading for Broadway. The Muppets face many obstacles as they try to make their way in New York City.

Old Yeller and ***20,000 Leagues Under the Sea***. Walt Disney Home Video.

These are just two of the twelve great live-action classics from Walt Disney's Studio Film Collection that are on the rental shelves.

♥

When Jake Berman was sick any Barney video made him feel better.

One Hundred and One Dalmations. Walt Disney Home Video.

This animated movie features Pongo and Perdita and their puppies, whom Cruella De Ville kidnaps to make a fur coat. Pongo and Perdita come to the rescue—comedy and suspense!

Paul Bunyon. SVS, Inc.

Jonathan Winters brings his own lunatic narrative style to this tale. The illustrations by Rick Mayerowitz are comical and really capture the atmosphere of a logging camp.

Pecos Bill. Rabbit Ears Productions / Uni Distribution, (800) 243-4504.

From the Rabbit Ears storytelling series. The narrative script is just a jumping-off point for Robin Williams, who gives hilarious voice to illustrator Tim Raglin's comic characters. Ry Cooder's music has just the right touch.

The Point. VES.

Ringo Starr narrates this feature about a boy who is exiled from society because his head is not pointed, but soon discovers you don't need "a point to have a point." This video includes a wonderful score by Harry Nilson.

Preschool Power! Jacket Flips and Other Tips. Concept Associates.

"I can do it on my own. You can do it once you've been shown." Kids ages two and up learn by watching their peers demonstrate easy ways to don their jackets, zip their zippers, and take care of their pets. Great for a child who's lonely in bed.

Raggedy Ann and Andy. Playhouse Video.

This imaginative animated film, based on the original Johnny Gruelle stories, is a treat.

Rain Forest Rap. World Wildlife Fund, P. O. Box 4866, Hampden Post Office, Baltimore, MD 21211, or call (301) 338-6951.

The tropical rain forest and the exotic creatures that live there are the stars of this ecovideo, which depicts the fabulous and unique ecosystem that is in so much danger of disappearing.

The Red Balloon. Children's Treasures / Nelson Entertainment.

A Grand Prize winner at the Cannes Film Festival, Albert Lamorisse's film about a lonely boy and a friendly red balloon is a timeless classic.

The Red Shoes. Family Home Entertainment.

An updated version of the classic fairy tale, this story is narrated by Ossie Davis and takes place in Harlem.

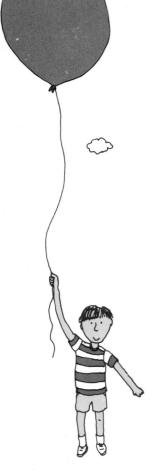

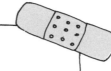

The Robert McCloskey Library. Children's Circle, (800) KIDS-VID.

Includes *Lentil*, *Blueberries for Sal*, *Make Way for Ducklings*, and *Burt Dow: Deep Water Man*. Expressive music and narration complement the package.

The Rocketeer. Walt Disney Home Video.

The adventures of a young man who discovers a top-secret project that allows him to fly. All in all, it's good children's entertainment.

Rover Dangerfield. Warner Home Video.

An animated canine, eyes bulging, loosens his red tie on the streets of Las Vegas.

Sebastian's Caribbean Jamboree. Walt Disney Home Video.

Your child will love this new Disney video starring Sam Wright, the human alter ego of Sebastian the Crab from *The Little Mermaid* (also available on Walt Disney Home Video). Crowd-shy Sebastian, seen in animated bits, turns the microphone over to the multitalented Wright, who sings and dances his way through Caribbean-flavored tunes.

The Secret Garden. Playhouse Video.

For those of you who don't want to mortgage the ranch to see the Broadway musical, this superior BBC live-action version is the perfect substitute.

Sesame Street. Random House Home Video.

A mere glimpse of *Sesame Street* on video will be enough to convince you of its magic. *Elmo's Sing-Along Guessing Game* is a half hour of mischief; *Big Bird in Japan* offers a certain large yellow bird lost in Tokyo; and *Don't Eat the Pictures* finds the whole gang locked overnight in the Metropolitan Museum of Art.

The Shaggy Dog. RCA.

A boy finds a ring that turns him into a sheep dog—a big problem for his dad who's allergic to dogs! The sequel, *The Shaggy D.A.* (Walt Disney Home Video), tells the story of a man who is running for district attorney, only to be turned into a sheep dog by an ancient ring that he finds.

Sing Yourself Silly. Random House Home Video.

Enjoy songs from *Sesame Street*, with Madeline Kahn, Jane Curtin, and John Candy, among other celebrities.

Still Life. Seventh Generation Environmental Video Collection, (800) 456-1177.

The Royal Ballet and narrator Jeremy Irons explore the plight of endangered animals at the Penguin Cafe. Other imaginative environmentally themed videos are also available.

Stories to Remember. Hi-Tops Video.

This series presents famous people reading favorite nursery tales.

The Story of the Dancing Frog. Family Home Entertainment.

This story is adapted from Quentin Blake's book and uses his illustrations.

Thomas the Tank Engine. Strand VCI Entertainment, (800) 922-3827 and (800) GO-TRAIN.

The live-action animation series from England about the adventures of the little "puffer-belly" trains with narration by Ringo Starr.

Wee Sing in Sillyville. Price Stern Sloan Video.

With their friend Silly Whim and lots of sing-along songs, a boy and a girl living in a coloring book help bring together the feuding Yellow Spurtlegurgles and Blue Twirlypops, and all the other crayon colors.

Willy Wonka and the Chocolate Factory. Warner Home Video.

Gene Wilder stars as Willy Wonka, the mysterious owner of a chocolate factory who holds a contest in which five winners are awarded a tour of his plant and a lifetime supply of chocolate. The real purpose of the contest—to find an honest boy who will inherit the chocolate factory.

Winnie-the-Pooh. Playhouse Video.

Some original spins on Winnie-the-Pooh with Ernest H. Shepard's original illustrations are now available.

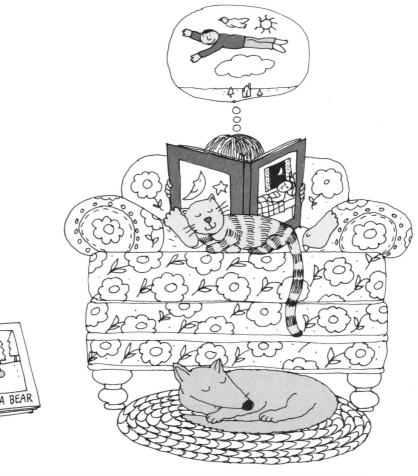

Comfort Foods ♥

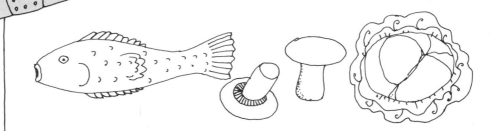

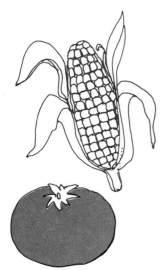

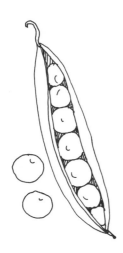

Most experts agree that when your child isn't feeling well and isn't hungry, even though a parent's normal urge is to force him to eat, that is not necessarily the best thing to do. Karen Borgie, Clinical Dietitian, Childrens Hospital Los Angeles, suggests, "Avoid making an issue out of eating. When a child gets hungry enough, he's going to eat. You can't manufacture hunger just by putting something in front of a child." Besides, refusing to eat is a great attention-getting device because most moms become unglued when sick kids don't eat.

Dr. Waldstein agrees. "Parents feel that they don't have much control over making sure their child gets better. The one thing they figure they *can* control is getting their child to eat. But most often this is unnecessary, although there will be times when getting your child to drink enough will be important." Children who are in the beginnings of a flu or other childhood disease will often "lose their appetite because of fatigue, side effects of medications, nausea, or other symptoms. When this happens, parents often panic, though a child can actually go for a few days without regular meals. So instead of becoming anxious, parents might decrease their expectations of what their child should eat and parents should support and praise whatever their child consumes," explains Dr. Waldstein.

What else can a parent do? "When a child is sick," says Karen Borgie, "he is already anxious, and feeling your anxiety because he's not eating will only make him worse. When it comes time for meals, give your child choices within some structure. 'Would you like chicken soup with noodles or rice?' or 'Would you like to help make up the menu for the day?' makes him feel like he has some control over his life."

Turning eating into a kind of game is sometimes successful with young children. Some parents of younger children have instituted a system of "Red Light, Green Light" patterned after the popular game. In this version, foods that are forbidden (either for allergic or health reasons) are "red light" foods. Foods called "yellow light" foods need a parent's permission to be eaten. For example, if your child has diarrhea and the doctor has ordered no salads for the week, salads become "yellow light" foods for that week. The "green light" foods are those that have been approved by doctor and parent. Your child may eat "green light" foods without special permission.

After your child has been home for a few days and is recovering, what he will need is to eat healthy food instead of empty calories. For example, the most important thing for a child to do when he has a stomach virus is to drink lots of fluids. "Fluids" means water, juice, and clear soups. After a few days of a

liquid diet, "introduce foods slowly and in small portions," continues Borgie. "When the child begins to eat again, try to make certain that the bulk of the foods you give him are things that slide down easily, that are easy to swallow, easy to chew, easy to digest—yogurts and healthy shakes and those kinds of things. Salads and raw vegetables are probably not going to be well accepted by a child who is recovering." You may also find that a child on the road to recovery may be better off eating five or six smaller meals rather than three large meals during the day. "All foods provide energy," explains Borgie. "But when a child is sick, what tastes good to him is probably something familiar, served in small portions in a pleasant atmosphere."

When your child gets well. celebrate with a special cake. Such a celebration is as important as any birthday!

Remember that this is not the time to make major changes in your child's diet. If there are foods that he has always loved (and your doctor says he can eat), this is the time to make them for him. If your child is feeling well enough to get out of bed, this may also be the time for the two of you to prepare food together. "Kids are much more willing to try something they have participated in making," explains Borgie.

As you look through the recipes in the following section, you will find that most of them are indeed "comfort foods." We're not sure why children who are sick love Jell-O, or mashed potatoes, or that universal favorite, chicken soup. (We asked Karen Borgie why chicken soup works so well when a child is sick. She said, "Chicken soup is fluid, it's light, it has carbohydrates, and it has protein. And believe it or not, the fact that it's warm and tastes good makes children feel better.") But we are hopeful that our collection of dishes will make your child happier in his recovery. The recipes are simple to prepare and made with both nutrition and taste in mind. And remember, always check with your doctor as to your child's diet when he is ill.

When your child is in bed, it's natural to bring him his meal on a tray. Making the tray more attractive, and serving the meals in ingenious ways, will go a long way in helping your child eat and enjoy his meals.

One of the most clever presentations of children's food that we've seen was at the Four Seasons Resort Wailea on Maui, in Hawaii. Their children's buffet, designed by Bill Miller, offered a child's delight. We have adapted his ideas for you to use on your child's bed trays.

★ Serve colorful fruits and vegetables in unusual containers.

★ Make pancakes or waffles in different shapes and serve them in dishes that match. Serve the syrup in a small plastic sand pail.

♥

Robert and Alec Bewkes had special place mats for when they were sick. They had clown faces on them with noses you could honk!

★ Cover the tray with a plastic place mat.

★ Fresh flowers in a small vase always brighten a bed tray.

★ TV trays, particularly those decorated with cartoon figures or other recognizable characters, are perfect for serving miniature sandwiches.

★ Plastic toy dump trucks (about 5 inches high) are perfect for holding fun-pack individual boxes of dry cereals.

★ Dot your tray with miniature dolls, trains, and other toys.

★ Plastic tug boats or other such bathtub boats hold fruit, muffins, or breads.

★ Use colored paper napkins and colored plastic flatware. (This is a great idea because you don't have to worry about washing utensils to keep other family members from becoming infected with your child's illness. Use paper cups for the same reason.)

♥
Remy Weber has kept a list throughout the years (he is now sixteen) of his favorite "sick-in-bed foods." Besides the inevitable chicken soup, his list includes egg creams, orange juice spritzers, chocolate pudding, granola with chopped apples and french vanilla yogurt, grapefruit with maple syrup granules, and matzo spread with honey and butter.

★ Serve hot drinks or soups in a small thermos. (The kind that come in small lunch boxes work well.) If your child doesn't finish the contents of the thermos, he can keep it by his bedside—nice and warm—and you won't have to prepare another serving.

RECIPE LIST

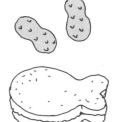

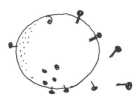

VEGETABLES   150

DESSERTS   152

♥

When Joni Staigers was faced with getting liquids into her sick children's tummies and she found the going rough, she devised two foolproof methods. For daughter Megan, she prepared tea parties and served the liquids in little teacups (Megan's sick dolls got to drink, of course). As for her son Garrett, he was crazy about crazy straws.

The following recipes represent a collection from our families, our friends, and some of the best cooks we know. Please remember that none of these are meant to be a substitute for your doctor's advice. Always check with your doctor for his recommendations as to what your child may or may not eat.

In this section you will find what we call "comfort foods." While some foods may be more of a comfort than others to your child, nevertheless they are the foods that make you feel good both in your tummy and in your heart. There is something about hot tea with honey, rice pudding, cinnamon toast, mashed potatoes, and macaroni and cheese that makes you feel better. And then of course there is chicken soup, which works wonders on a variety of illnesses. As a matter of fact, everyone we talked to suggested chicken soup as a comfort food, and nearly everyone had their own favorite recipe for their own favorite chicken soup. While we of course acknowledge that every mother's chicken soup is the best, we couldn't include all the chicken soup recipes of all the mothers we know. Therefore, you will find five chicken soup recipes in this book. Each one is a little different, each one has a favorite ingredient that gives it its own personality and taste, and each one holds a promise to make your child feel better.

Please note: Some of our recipes include raw egg yolks. There has recently been an increase in the incidence of salmonella-related, food-borne illness in the United States; if you have any concerns at all about the possible contamination of eggs available in your area, you should avoid using these recipes.

ESTHER'S GOGLE-MOGLE

Annie's mom made this drink for her whenever a sore throat appeared. It soothed the throat immediately and somehow had magical powers to soothe the soul as well.

2 egg yolks
3 tablespoons sugar
1 cup very hot milk

Beat the egg yolks very well, until they are light and yellow. Add the sugar and beat again until very smooth. Pour into a large mug and fill with the hot milk. Stir constantly to avoid cooking the yolks. Serve.

Variation: Add a tablespoon of cocoa at the time you add the sugar.

SERVES 1

CHOCOLATE EGGNOG

1 egg white
1 teaspoon cocoa powder
1 tablespoon honey
1 egg yolk, beaten
1 cup milk

Beat the egg white until stiff. In a blender, mix the cocoa, honey, and egg yolk. Fold the egg white into the cocoa-honey blend. Now, slowly add the milk, stirring all the time. Serve immediately.

SERVES 1

FEEL BETTER EGGNOG

1 egg
1 teaspoon honey or pineapple juice
3 drops vanilla extract
1 cup milk
Nutmeg

Beat the egg. Combine the honey and the vanilla in a small saucepan. Warm over low heat, stirring constantly. Add the beaten egg and mix well. Pour into a glass. Add the milk, stir well, and top with a grind or two of nutmeg.

SERVES 1

SUPERHERO MILK

3 tablespoons malted milk powder
1 cup milk

Combine the malted milk powder and the milk in a saucepan. Heat gently.

SERVES 1

GET BETTER JUICE

½ cup grapefruit juice
½ cup pineapple juice
½ cup apple juice
1 tablespoon honey
½ tablespoon orange marmalade

Combine the juices, honey, and marmalade. Stir or blend until thoroughly mixed. Strain and drink.

SERVES 1

HEAVENLY DRINK

1 cup orange juice
Drops of lemon juice to taste
1 teaspoon honey

Mix the orange juice and the lemon juice. Now add the honey. Heat gently, stirring, until the honey dissolves.

SERVES 1

❤
Becca Bloom used to drink hot lemonade whenever she was sick. Her mom, Ruth, would boil 2 cups of water, add the juice of one lemon, and stir in 1 tablespoon of honey, then serve it to Becca in a big mug.

134

♥

Ginger tea is good for an upset stomach as well as for a cold.

♥

To make a quick single-serving of fruit ice, freeze 1 cup of your favorite fruit (strawberries, bananas, blueberries). Place the frozen fruit in a food processor with ½ teaspoon of lemon juice and blend. Eat immediately.

CINNAMON TEA

1 teaspoon honey
1 tablespoon lemon juice
1 cup very hot lemon herb tea or water
Twist of lemon peel
Ground cinnamon, nutmeg, or cloves

In a mug, stir the honey and lemon juice together with a long-handled metal spoon. Leave the spoon in the mug and pour in the tea. Float the lemon peel and sprinkle the cinnamon on top.

SERVES 1

TEA THYME

Good for coughs and sore throats.

1 teaspoon dried thyme
1 cup boiling water
1 teaspoon honey
Drop of lemon juice

Put the thyme in a mug. Add the boiling water. Let steep for 5 minutes or more. Strain and return to the mug. Stir in the honey to dissolve and add the lemon juice.

SERVES 1

TROPICAL FRAPPÉ

1 cup mixed fresh fruit juices or nectars (any combination of your choice: orange and cranberry, orange and pineapple, orange and apricot)
½ cup plain low-fat yogurt

Mix the juices of your choice. Freeze in ice cube trays (1 cup of liquid makes 8 ice cubes). Place 8 frozen cubes in a large bowl and beat with an electric mixer or place in a food processor and using the steel blade, process until slushy.
Proceed as follows:
If using a mixer, place the bowl in the freezer for 30 minutes, remove, and beat again. Add the yogurt and beat.

If using a food processor, add the yogurt and blend.
Serve in a frozen glass or goblet. Garnish with mint leaves or fresh fruit.

SERVES 1

LEMON FREEZER

3 cups plain low-fat yogurt
½ teaspoon vanilla extract
1 teaspoon grated lemon zest
2 teaspoons sugar

Combine all the ingredients in a bowl. Whip until well mixed. Freeze. Serve in small bowls and eat with a spoon.

SERVES 6

FRUIT MILK SHAKE

⅔ cup fruit juice or a combination of fruit juices (see below)
1⅓ cups cold milk
2 ice cubes

Combine all the ingredients in a blender and blend until smooth and frothy. Try combining orange and white grape juices, orange and pineapple juices, grapefruit and cranberry juices, or orange juice whipped with banana to make your own favorite shake.

SERVES 1

HOT CRANBERRY JUICE

1 cup cranberry juice
1 slice lemon
Pinch of ground cloves
Honey to taste or 1 cinnamon stick (optional)

Combine all the ingredients in an enamel or nonreactive saucepan. Simmer over low heat. Do not boil.

SERVES 1

HOT CHOCOLATE I

*1 ounce (1 square) unsweetened
    chocolate*
*1 tablespoon unsweetened cocoa
    powder*
5 tablespoons sugar
1½ cups milk
1 cup half-and-half

Combine the chocolate, cocoa, and sugar in a saucepan. Heat over medium heat. Stir frequently until the chocolate is melted and the sugar is dissolved. Stirring, add the milk and half-and-half. Heat until piping hot, but not boiling. Pour the mixture into a blender and whip until light and frothy. Pour into mugs and serve immediately.

SERVES 3 TO 4

HOT CHOCOLATE II

*1½ to 2 ounces (1½ to 2 squares)
    unsweetened chocolate*
1 cup boiling water
3 cups milk
1 vanilla bean
¼ cup sugar
⅛ teaspoon salt
¼ cup whipped cream (optional)
4 cinnamon sticks (optional)

Melt the chocolate in the top of a double boiler with the boiling water. Over direct heat, bring the mixture to the point where it begins to foam up. Quickly lift the top of the double boiler from the heat. Let the liquid recede. Repeat the foaming and receding process three or four times in all.

Pour the milk into a saucepan and add the vanilla bean. Scald the milk. Dissolve the sugar and the salt in the milk. Remove the vanilla bean. Pour the hot milk mixture over the smooth chocolate mixture. Beat well with a wire whisk.

If you desire, fold the whipped cream into the mixture or top the hot chocolate with whipped cream in each cup. Another option—before serving, place a cinnamon stick in each cup.

SERVES 4

FRUIT SMOOTHIE

*2 cups fruit, fresh or frozen (bananas,
    strawberries, and melon are
    nice singly or in combination)*
*2 cups fruit juice (orange, grapefruit,
    or cranberry—choose one that
    mixes well with the fruit you're
    using)*
1¼ cups vanilla low-fat yogurt

Combine all the ingredients in a blender, mixing until thick and smooth.

SERVES 2

GRAPE SURPRISE

3 cups grape juice
1 cup pineapple juice
½ cup vanilla low-fat yogurt
2 ice cubes

Combine the juices and the yogurt in a blender. Add the ice and blend until the mixture thickens.

SERVES 2

WARM MOON GLOW

2 cups milk
Pinch of ground ginger
Pinch of ground cinnamon
¼ teaspoon vanilla extract
1 teaspoon honey (or to taste)

Combine all the ingredients in a saucepan. Heat gently—be careful not to boil. Stir several times. This won't need much sweetening, since warm milk is naturally sweet. Pour into mugs and serve at once.

SERVES 1 TO 2

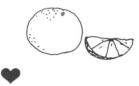

♥

Peel and cut up overripe fruit. Freeze in freezer bags. Use as needed.

♥

Stacey Holston's mom, Bobbie, made Stacey and her sister orange freezies with juice and sherbet to soothe a sore throat.

SNACKS

PEANUT DIP

⅔ cup crunchy peanut butter
6 tablespoons brown sugar
½ cup lemon juice

Combine all the ingredients in a bowl. Refrigerate at least 2 to 4 hours before serving.

Serve with celery sticks, carrot sticks, cucumber sticks, or zucchini sticks.

MAKES APPROXIMATELY 1 CUP

HONEY MILK TOAST

1 cup milk
1 slice bread
Butter
Honey

Gently heat the milk. While the milk is heating, toast the bread, butter it on one side, and cut it into four pieces. Pour the hot milk into a warm bowl. Float the buttered toast pieces in the hot milk and drizzle honey over them. Eat with a spoon.

SERVES 1

Joan Talarico's kids, Annie and Nicholas, both loved to have tea and cinnamon toast served to them in bed on trays. Even medication served on a tray makes taking pills or syrups more palatable.

FAVORITE EASY CINNAMON TOAST

Butter, at room temperature
8 slices white bread
3 tablespoons sugar
½ teaspoon ground cinnamon

Spread butter generously on the bread slices and place them on a cookie sheet. Combine the sugar and the cinnamon. Sprinkle a tablespoon of the cinnamon sugar on each slice. Place the bread in the oven 6 to 8 inches from the broiler. Broil until the cinnamon sugar is bubbly, but remove before the crusts are brown. Cool, then cut into triangles.

SERVES 4 TO 8, DEPENDING ON APPETITE

GRANOLA

3 cups rolled oats
½ cup wheat germ
¾ cup sunflower seeds
1½ cups shredded unsweetened coconut
½ cup sesame seeds
¼ cup toasted bran
¾ cup honey
¾ cup safflower or canola oil
1 teaspoon vanilla extract
1½ cup raisins

Preheat the oven to 400°F.

Mix the dry ingredients in a bowl. In a small saucepan, heat the honey and the oil until they can be mixed together. Add the vanilla. Pour the honey-oil mixture over the dry ingredients and mix until everything is coated. Spread on a cookie sheet and bake in the oven.

Using a spatula, keep turning the mixture until it is toasted throughout. Put into a large clean bowl and add the raisins (they will burn if added when cooking). Store in jars.

MAKES ABOUT 8 CUPS

SKORDALIA

Joan Talarico's mother-in-law swears by the natural antibiotic properties of garlic. The Greek people make a spread called *skordalia* that can be put on crackers or toast. If your child enjoys garlic, *skordalia* is the thing to make.

10 cloves garlic
⅓ cup white vinegar
1 cup soft white bread crumbs moistened with water or 1 mashed potato
1½ cups mixed vegetable and olive oil
1 egg yolk

Peel the garlic and place in a blender or a food processor with the vinegar. Blend until smooth. Add the bread crumbs and continue to blend. Slowly add the oil. Once the mixture has reached the consistency of a thick mayonnaise, add the egg yolk and blend until well mixed.

MAKES 2 TO 3 CUPS

GO FISH

10 slices thinly sliced firm white bread
1 cup chunky peanut butter
¼ cup vegetable oil

Preheat the oven to 350°F. Trim the crusts from the bread slices and set aside. Use a fish-shaped cookie cutter to cut shapes out of the bread. Reserve the scraps. Place the fish flat on a baking sheet. Toast lightly in the oven.

Place the trimmed crusts and the bread scraps on another baking sheet and bake until golden brown. Place in a food processor or a blender. Blend to make fine bread crumbs. Remove the crumbs to a shallow bowl.

Heat the peanut butter and the oil in a small saucepan until blended and warm. Dip the toasted fish completely into the peanut butter mixture and then coat with the bread crumbs. Let the fish dry flat on a baking sheet. Store in an airtight container.

MAKES 10 TO 48 FISH, DEPENDING ON THE SIZE OF YOUR COOKIE CUTTER

SWEET POTATO CHIPS

This is one of our favorite recipes from the *Penny Whistle Christmas Party Book*.

Heat 3 inches of vegetable oil in a wok to 375°F. Peel sweet potatoes and slice them on a slicer or in a food processor to the desired thickness. Fry until crisp. Drain on paper towels.

Season with salt, or for a more interesting taste (says our friend Don Ernstein of Wonderful Foods in Los Angeles), season with super-fine sugar and cinnamon.

FRUIT

YOGURT AND FRUIT

½ cup plain nonfat yogurt
½ cup puréed fresh strawberries or bananas or ¼ cup each
Honey to taste (optional)

Mix together the yogurt and the puréed fruit in a bowl. You can add honey if you like.

SERVES 1

APPLES BAKED IN CRANBERRY JUICE

4 small to medium cooking apples
¼ cup sugar
½ cup brown sugar
½ teaspoon ground cinnamon
¼ cup dried cranberries
1 cup cranberry juice
1 tablespoon margarine or butter

Preheat the oven to 350°F. Core the apples, removing the stem and seeds but leaving the bottoms intact by at least ¾ inch. Place the apples in a glass baking dish.

In a small bowl, combine the sugars, cinnamon, and cranberries. Stuff the cored apples with the sugar mixture. Pour the cranberry juice around the apples. Top each apple with a pat of margarine. Cover the dish with aluminum foil and bake the apples for 30 to 40 minutes, depending on the size of the apples, until tender. Do not overbake.

Carefully remove the apples from the baking dish and place on a serving plate. Pour the juice into a small nonreactive saucepan and boil until reduced to about ½ cup, or until it becomes a little syrupy. Drizzle over the apples. Serve slightly warm or chilled.

SERVES 4

♥

Serve cut-up fruit in ice-cream cones for a different presentation. Sprinkle granola or crushed granola bars on top. You can also mix cut-up fruit with low-fat ricotta or cottage cheese and serve in an ice-cream cone or in a bowl.

The slow-cooking method of a Crockpot is ideal for making applesauce.

APPLESAUCE

2½ pounds tart apples
½ cup honey
¼ teaspoon ground cinnamon

Peel and core the apples. Slice the apples into quarters. Place the quartered apples in a large saucepan. Cover with water. Bring to a boil, reduce the heat, and simmer for 10 minutes. With a potato masher, crush the apples thoroughly. Add the honey and the cinnamon. Simmer for 15 to 20 minutes longer. Cool. Freeze or store in the refrigerator.

Variations: (1) Combine with 1 cup puréed apricots or raspberries. (2) Combine with 1 cup crushed pineapple and 1 teaspoon ground ginger. (3) Combine with 2 cups cranberry sauce.

MAKES ABOUT 1 QUART

BAKED APPLES

6 large apples (Rome Beauties or
    York Imperials work well)
1 cup sugar
2 cups boiling water
1 cinnamon stick
½ cup raisins or dried cherries

Preheat the oven to 375°F. Core each of the apples to within ½ inch of its base. Arrange the apples in a buttered baking dish.

Combine the sugar, water, and cinnamon stick in a saucepan. Stir to dissolve the sugar and bring to a boil. Boil rapidly until the mixture becomes a thin syrup, about 8 minutes.

Stuff the centers of the apples with the raisins. Remove the cinnamon stick from the syrup. Pour the syrup over the apples. Bake in the middle of the oven for 40 minutes or until the apples are soft to the touch but not falling apart.

Transfer the apples to serving dishes and pour the syrup remaining in the baking dish over them.

SERVES 6

SPICY APPLESAUCE

8 cooking apples (Pippins or Granny
    Smiths are a good choice)
½ cup unsweetened apple juice
1 tablespoon peeled, minced fresh
    ginger
1½ teaspoons ground cinnamon
½ teaspoon each ground allspice,
    ground cloves, and crushed
    anise seeds
Lemon juice to taste

Peel and core the apples. Cut the apples into small chunks. Place all the ingredients except the lemon juice in a large saucepan. Cover with a tight-fitting lid. Over medium heat, cook the apples until tender. Leave chunky. Add lemon juice to taste. Serve warm or at room temperature.

SERVES 4

BANANA SPLIT

1 banana, peeled
½ cup cottage cheese
Blueberries or strawberries, rinsed,
    hulled, and cut into small pieces

Slice the banana lengthwise in half. In a bowl, combine the cottage cheese and the berries. (This sweetens the cheese.) Blend well. Place one "scoop" of cottage cheese on each banana half.

SERVES 1

HOT CLOVE ORANGES

1 medium juice orange, peeled and
    sliced
Pinch of ground cloves
Honey
Lemon drops (candy)

Preheat the oven to 300°F.
Place the orange slices flat in a glass baking dish or pie pan. Sprinkle with cloves. Spoon the honey and the lemon drops over the orange slices and bake for 10 minutes.

SERVES 1

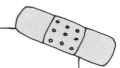

BREAD

POPOVERS

3 eggs
1½ cups milk
1 tablespoon melted butter
1 teaspoon salt
1½ cups unbleached all-purpose flour

Preheat the oven to 400°F. Butter a twelve-cup muffin tin.

Beat all the ingredients together until smooth. Fill the muffin cups two-thirds full. Bake for 45 minutes. Score the top of each muffin. Return the muffin tin to the oven for 5 to 10 minutes. Serve hot with your favorite jam and butter.

MAKES 12 POPOVERS

ORANGE YOGURT PANCAKES WITH STRAWBERRIES

1 pint strawberries, rinsed, hulled,
*   and sliced*
2 tablespoons sugar
Chopped zest of 1 orange
½ cup orange juice
3 tablespoons sugar
¾ cup plain low-fat yogurt
1 large egg
2 tablespoons melted unsalted butter
1 cup all-purpose flour
1 teaspoon baking soda
½ teaspoon baking powder
¼ teaspoon salt
4 tablespoons melted unsalted butter,
*   for the griddle*
4 tablespoons plain low-fat yogurt,
*   for garnish*
Warm maple syrup

In a bowl, toss the sliced strawberries with the 2 tablespoons sugar. In a large mixing bowl, combine the orange zest, orange juice, 3 tablespoons sugar, yogurt, egg, and 2 tablespoons melted butter. Beat until well mixed. Stir in the flour, baking soda, baking powder, and salt. Stir the mixture well, until the batter is thick.

Heat a griddle or a large skillet. When the griddle is hot, brush it with some melted butter. Spoon the batter onto the griddle and spread to form a 3-inch-round pancake. Cook 1 to 2 minutes on each side. Transfer to an ovenproof platter. (This may be done up to an hour in advance.)

Warm the pancakes for approximately 5 minutes in a preheated 350°F oven before serving.

Garnish the pancakes with yogurt. Serve with the sliced strawberries and warm maple syrup!

MAKES A DOZEN MEDIUM-SIZE PANCAKES

MONTANA APPLE PANCAKE

2 apples
2 eggs
2 cups all-purpose flour
3 teaspoons baking powder
½ teaspoon salt
3 tablespoons sugar
1⅓ cups milk
½ teaspoon vanilla extract
½ teaspoon ground cinnamon
3 tablespoons margarine

Preheat the oven to 450°F.

Peel, core, and cut up the apples. Combine all the other ingredients, except the margarine. Mix until moist. Melt the margarine in a 12-inch ovenproof frying pan. Place the apples in the pan. Cover with the batter. Place the pan in the oven and bake the pancake, turning it once after 10 to 15 minutes. Bake until brown. Sprinkle the pancake with brown sugar and serve with maple syrup.

SERVES 2 TO 4

EASY BAKED APPLE PANCAKE

3 apples, peeled, cored, and sliced
    (Pippins or Granny Smiths
    are best)
Juice of 1 lemon
1 tablespoon butter or margarine
4 eggs
Pinch of grated nutmeg
½ cup all-purpose flour
½ teaspoon salt
½ cup milk
¼ teaspoon vanilla extract
2 tablespoons butter or margarine
1 teaspoon powdered sugar
½ teaspoon fresh lemon juice

Preheat the oven to 400°F.

Cover the apple slices with the juice of one lemon. Melt the 1 tablespoon butter in a skillet. Over low heat, sauté the apples until they are soft and lightly browned. Set aside.

Beat the eggs with the nutmeg in a bowl. Sift the flour and salt together into a small bowl. Add to the eggs and beat constantly. Gradually add the milk. Blend until the batter is smooth. Stir in the vanilla.

In an ovenproof frying pan, melt the 2 tablespoons butter. Pour the batter into the pan and place the apples in the middle. Put the pan in the oven and bake the pancake for 15 minutes at 400°F. Lower the oven temperature to 350°F and bake until the pancake rises and is fluffy (about 5 minutes). Your oven temperature should be exact to make this work.

Remove the pancake from the oven. Sprinkle with powdered sugar and fresh lemon juice, and serve immediately. Cut into wedges or scoop to serve.

SERVES 4

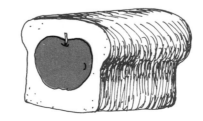

APPLE QUICK BREAD

¾ cup sugar
⅓ cup margarine or butter, softened
1 egg
2 cups all-purpose flour
1 teaspoon baking powder
½ teaspoon baking soda
⅓ cup orange juice
2 apples, peeled, cored, and chopped
½ cup dried cherries, dried cranberries,
    or raisins

Preheat the oven to 350°F. Grease a 9-by-5-inch loaf pan.

Cream the sugar and margarine together in a mixing bowl. Add the egg and beat well. In a separate mixing bowl, combine the flour, baking powder, and baking soda. Add the dry ingredients alternately with the orange juice to the egg mixture. Mix until slightly moistened. Stir in the apples and the cherries.

Turn the mixture into the prepared loaf pan. Bake for 1 hour. Place the pan on a wire rack to cool for 10 minutes. Remove the loaf from the pan. Be sure to cool the bread completely before serving.

MAKES 1 LOAF

COTTAGE CHEESE PANCAKES

1 cup cottage cheese
6 eggs, well beaten
6 tablespoons all-purpose flour, sifted
6 tablespoons melted butter
Pinch of salt

Rub the cottage cheese through a fine sieve. Stir in the eggs and mix thoroughly. Add the sifted flour, the melted butter, and a pinch of salt. Beat until well blended.

Drop the batter by the spoonful onto a buttered hot griddle. Brown, turning the pancakes only once.

Serve with butter, jam, or low-fat yogurt.

**MAKES APPROXIMATELY
20 HALF-DOLLAR-SIZE PANCAKES**

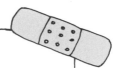

BAKING POWDER BISCUITS

2 cups all-purpose flour
2 teaspoons baking powder
2 teaspoons sugar
6 tablespoons cold margarine
¾ cup milk

Preheat the oven to 450°F.

Mix the flour, baking powder, and sugar together. Add the margarine. Cut with a pastry blender until the dough is fine but pebbly. Add the milk quickly, mixing until the dough is just moistened. Drop the dough onto a greased cookie sheet. Bake for 12 to 15 minutes. If you like, sprinkle with sugar before baking.

MAKES 10 TO 12 BISCUITS

BASIC CREPE RECIPE

½ cup all-purpose flour
⅓ teaspoon sugar
Pinch of salt
1 egg
½ cup milk
2 teaspoons melted and cooled butter
    or margarine

Sift the flour, sugar, and salt together into a mixing bowl. Add the egg and mix thoroughly to form a thick paste. Add the milk gradually, beating thoroughly. Add the melted and cooled butter. Add whatever flavoring you wish and mix. Allow the batter to stand for at least 1 hour. (If the crepe batter seems too thick when you are ready to cook, a small amount of liquid can be added. The consistency of the batter should be that of heavy cream.)

Heat a small crepe pan that is 5 or 6 inches across the bottom. Brush with butter and when the butter is hot, but not smoking, lift the pan off the heat and pour in 1½ to 2 tablespoons of batter. Swirl quickly to cover the bottom of the pan. Return the pan to the heat. Turn the crepe when it is golden brown (after about 1 minute). Cook on the reverse side for about half a minute.

Turn the crepe out onto a clean kitchen towel or paper towels. Continue cooking the crepes, adding butter to the pan as needed. Stack the crepes on a plate and keep them warm in a low oven if they are to be used immediately. Or, if they are to be held, cool, stack with waxed paper between each, and cover. To freeze, wrap in aluminum foil, freezer paper, or freezer bags, and freeze immediately. Remove from the freezer and thaw at room temperature.

Try preparing your crepes as follows: Fill with low-fat ricotta cheese and top with tomato sauce; fill with slices of baked apple (see page 138); fill with steamed spinach, cubes of roasted chicken (see page 148), and top with melted cheese; fill with frozen yogurt and top with sliced strawberries, bananas, or blueberries; fill with steamed broccoli and melted cheese. Experiment with your own combinations.

SERVES 2

ALL-SEASON PUMPKIN BREAD

2 cups all-purpose flour
1 cup sugar
1 cup canned pumpkin purée
    (not pumpkin pie filling)
3 eggs
1 teaspoon baking powder
⅓ cup vegetable oil
2 teaspoons ground cinnamon
½ teaspoon ground cloves
Pinch of ground nutmeg
½ cup raisins

Preheat the oven to 350°F. Butter a 9-by-5-inch loaf pan.

In a large bowl, combine all the ingredients, stirring with a wooden spoon until well mixed. Pour the batter into the prepared pan. Bake for 40 to 50 minutes or until a toothpick inserted in the center comes out clean.

Cool the bread on a rack before removing from the pan. Wrap in a plastic bag and store at room temperature or in the refrigerator.

MAKES 1 LOAF

♥

In France, when Françoise Morison was young, her favorite comfort food was crepes sprinkled with brown sugar and rolled. Her family also served their crepes open with a fried egg and bacon, filled with chicken, broccoli, and bèchamel sauce, or filled with applesauce and topped with vanilla ice cream.

MAIN COURSES ✩

GARDEN PIZZA

1 (12-inch) Boboli, focaccio, or
    ready-to-bake pizza shell
1 cup shredded mozzarella cheese
½ cup tomato sauce
1½ teaspoons dried dill
½ teaspoon seasoned salt
½ teaspoon fines herbes
1½ teaspoons lemon juice
2 drops Tabasco
⅛ teaspoon garlic powder
Freshly ground black pepper to taste
Fresh, colorful chopped vegetables of
    your choice: tomatoes, mush-
    rooms, zucchini, green bell
    peppers, red bell peppers, black
    olives, radishes, broccoli florets,
    carrots

Preheat the oven to 450°F.

Place the pizza shell on a 12-inch pizza pan. Combine the cheese with the tomato sauce and all the seasonings. Spread over the shell. Sprinkle the chopped vegetables over the top. Heat in the oven until the cheese melts. Cut the pizza into small wedges. Serve.

SERVES 4

PIZZA MARGHERITA

1 pound tomatoes, peeled, or
    1 (16-ounce) can tomatoes,
    drained
2 tablespoons olive oil
1 onion, finely chopped
1 clove garlic, crushed
1 tablespoon tomato paste
½ teaspoon sugar
1 tablespoon chopped fresh basil
Salt and pepper to taste
1 (12-inch) Boboli, focaccio, or
    ready-to-bake pizza shell
2 tablespoons olive oil
4 ounces mozzarella cheese
6 to 8 fresh basil leaves

Make the tomato topping: Chop the tomatoes, if using fresh. In a medium saucepan, heat the 2 tablespoons oil. Add the onion and the garlic and cook until soft. Add the tomatoes, tomato paste, sugar, and chopped basil. Stir. Season to taste with salt and pepper. Cover the pan and simmer for 30 minutes, until the sauce is thick.

Preheat the oven to 450°F. Lightly grease a 12-inch pizza pan.

Place the pizza shell in the prepared pan and brush with 1 tablespoon of the oil. Spoon the tomato topping over the shell. Slice the cheese thinly and sprinkle over the tomato sauce.

Sprinkle with salt and pepper to taste, 2 or 3 basil leaves, and the remaining oil. Bake for 20 minutes, until the cheese has melted and the crust is crisp and golden. Garnish with the remaining basil leaves. Serve immediately.

SERVES 4

PIZZA FACES

2 ready-to-bake individual pizza shells
    or pita breads
¼ cup tomato sauce
6 to 8 processed Cheddar cheese slices
Alfalfa sprouts or grated carrot
Olive slices
Wide bell pepper strips
Herb sprigs

Preheat the oven to 450°F.

Spread the pizza shells with the tomato sauce. Arrange the cheese over the top. Place on a baking sheet and bake for 10 to 15 minutes, until the cheese is melted.

Give your child the baked pizza shells and the ingredients to make a pizza face on each shell, using alfalfa sprouts for the hair, olive slices for the eyes, bell pepper strips for the mouth, and herb sprigs for the nose.

SERVES 2

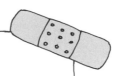

FOUR-CHEESE PIZZA

1 (12-inch) Boboli, focaccio, or
    ready-to-bake pizza shell
2 tablespoons olive oil
2 ounces ricotta cheese
2 ounces cubed mozzarella cheese
2 ounces cubed Fontina cheese
½ cup freshly grated Parmesan cheese
Salt and pepper to taste
Chopped green onion and freshly
    grated Parmesan cheese, for
    garnish

Preheat the oven to 450°F.

Brush the dough with 1 tablespoon of the oil. Spread the ricotta cheese and sprinkle with the remaining three cheeses. Season to taste with salt and pepper. Drizzle with the remaining oil.

Bake for 10 minutes, until the cheese is melted and the crust is crisp and golden. Garnish with green onion and additional Parmesan cheese.

SERVES 4

QUESADILLA

Butter
2 flour tortillas
Monterey Jack cheese
Sour cream (optional)
Salsa (optional)
Mild green chili peppers (optional)
Jalapeño peppers (optional)

Melt a pat of butter in a large skillet. Lay a flour tortilla in the pan and cover with thinly sliced Jack cheese. Place the other tortilla on top of the cheese. Cover the pan and cook over low heat until the cheese is almost melted. Flip the quesadilla over and brown the other side. Cut it like a pie and serve with sour cream and/or salsa. You can mix chopped mild green chili peppers in with the cheese, or if you like it hot, try it with sliced jalapeño peppers.

SERVES 1

FRENCH BREAD PIZZA

1 medium French bread loaf
2 tablespoons olive oil
1 (16-ounce) can tomatoes
Salt and pepper to taste
1 (6-ounce) can tuna in oil, drained
8 pimiento-stuffed olives
1 cup shredded Edam cheese
3 green onions, chopped

Preheat the oven to 450°F. Cut a slice from the top of the French loaf along the whole length. Scoop out most of the soft bread from the bottom portion (the soft bread and the lid will not be required but can be used for bread crumbs).

Brush the inside of the loaf with half the oil. Drain the tomatoes and save the juice. Brush the inside of the loaf with the tomato juice. Place the loaf on a baking sheet and bake for 10 minutes.

Chop the drained tomatoes and spoon half into the loaf. Season to taste with salt and pepper. Flake the tuna and spoon over the tomatoes and season again with salt and pepper.

Halve the olives and sprinkle on top. Sprinkle with the cheese. Return the loaf to the oven and bake for 15 minutes. Sprinkle with the chopped green onions and serve at once.

SERVES 2

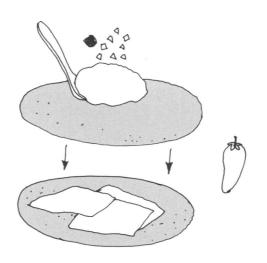

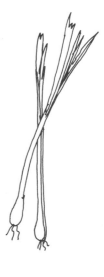

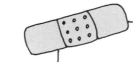

♥

For a child who faces an extended stay at home or even in the hospital, a pretend trip is an excellent diversion. Travel posters, special foods of that particular country (see The Penny Whistle Party Planner *and* Lunch Box Book *for ideas), and maybe even learning a little of the language can turn the flu into a vacation.*

BEELER BROTH

1 pound green beans, cut up
2 pounds zucchini, cut up
½ large bunch celery, washed and cut up
1 bunch fresh parsley
1 onion, coarsely chopped
1 tablespoon salt

Put all the ingredients in a saucepan. Add water to cover two-thirds of the vegetables. Bring to a boil. Reduce the heat, cover, and simmer for 30 minutes. Purée in a blender, food mill, or food processor and serve.

MAKES ABOUT 1 QUART

TOMATO SOUP

1 quart low-fat milk
1 small onion, thickly sliced
1 bay leaf
2 tablespoons butter
2 tablespoons all-purpose flour
1 teaspoon salt
Pinch of white pepper
1 (16-ounce) can Italian tomatoes, drained and mashed
1 tablespoon sugar (optional)

Scald the milk with the onion and the bay leaf. Cover and let stand for 10 to 15 minutes. Remove and discard the onion and the bay leaf. Melt the butter in a nonreactive saucepan. Stir in the flour and cook over moderately high heat until lightly colored. Pour in about 1 cup of the scalded milk and stir until thickened. Gradually add the rest of the milk. Season with the salt and a pinch of white pepper. Cook the tomatoes over medium heat in another saucepan until they begin to give off liquid. Add sugar if the tomatoes are too acid. Strain the tomatoes.

Add the strained tomatoes gradually to the thickened milk. Season to taste. Serve hot.

MAKES 2 LARGE BOWLS OR 4 SMALL BOWLS

MATZO BALLS

3 eggs
3½ cups water
1 small onion, diced and fried in 3 teaspoons oil in a small saucepan until brown
Pinch of salt
Pinch of ground cinnamon (optional)
Approximately ¾ cup matzo meal

Mix all the ingredients together except the matzo meal. Put in enough matzo meal to make a soft dough. The amount of matzo meal may vary depending on the size of your eggs. (Do not make it too hard.) Refrigerate for 20 to 30 minutes. Remove the dough from the refrigerator and form it into balls. Drop them into boiling salted water, reduce the heat, and simmer, covered, for 20 to 25 minutes. The matzo balls can be made ahead of time and kept in a covered dish. Drop the balls into hot soup when ready to serve. Do not put matzo balls into cold soup!

Use with any chicken soup, even canned.

MAKES ABOUT A DOZEN MATZO BALLS

SONI'S PENICILLIN CHICKEN SOUP

1 whole large chicken, giblets removed
1 onion, quartered
2 carrots, peeled and halved
2 stalks celery, washed
1 bay leaf
1 tablespoon salt
¼ teaspoon pepper
¼ cup fresh parsley sprigs
3 cloves garlic, halved

Place the chicken in the center of a large stockpot, and cover with cold water (3 quarts should do it). Bring to a boil, reduce the heat, and simmer until just tender, about 1½ hours. Add the onion, carrots, celery, bay leaf, salt, pepper, parsley, and garlic. Cook for about 1 hour. Remove the chicken and all the vege-

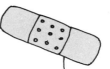

tables. (Annie throws out the bay leaf, saves the vegetables, and then creams them in the food processor. She adds them to the soup another day to make a kind of cream of vegetable soup.) Strain the broth. Chill in the refrigerator overnight. The next day remove the fat with a slotted spoon.

Serve the broth with noodles, rice, or Matzo Balls (page 144), or serve just the warm broth in a cup. The chicken can be shredded and added to the soup.

MAKES ABOUT 3 QUARTS

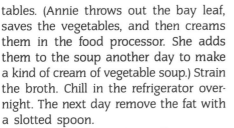

MICHELLE'S ALPHABET CHICKEN SOUP

2 leeks, well washed and sliced
1 tablespoon cider vinegar
1 cup margarine
1 carrot, peeled and chopped
2 stalks celery, washed
1 teaspoon kosher salt
½ teaspoon bell pepper
3 (14½-ounce) cans chicken broth
1 chicken breast, cooked, skinned, and shredded
2 cups cooked alphabet noodles

Place the leeks in a bowl with the vinegar and cover with water. Let sit for 30 minutes. Melt the margarine in a skillet and sauté the carrot, celery, kosher salt, and bell pepper. Add the leeks with a slotted spoon and cook for another 5 minutes.

Pour the chicken broth into a stockpot and add the vegetables and chicken. Simmer for about 30 minutes. Just before you are ready to serve, add the alphabet noodles.

MAKES APPROXIMATELY 1½ TO 2 QUARTS

AUNT IDA'S CHICKEN SOUP

"Natural" is Aunt Ida's favorite word. We're not sure what she means by "natural"—but we do know that when it comes to chicken soup made with kosher "naturally" fed chicken, hers is unbeatable and has made many a sore-throated child feel a lot better.

1 large kosher chicken (remove the insides but save the giblets)
2 carrots, peeled and cut up
2 stalks celery, washed and chopped
1 onion, quartered
2 leeks, well washed and sliced
A handful of fresh parsley
1 parsley root, peeled and diced
Salt to taste

Cut up the chicken, trim off the excess fat, and place (with the giblets) in a large stockpot. Cover with cold water just to the top of the meat (not too much!—about 3 quarts). Bring to a boil, reduce the heat, and simmer, uncovered, until the water looks pretty clear. Skim off the scum. Cover the pot and cook again on low heat for 1 hour. Now add all the vegetables, bring back to a boil, then reduce the heat and simmer for another 1½ hours. Taste to see if it needs salt. (Sometimes Annie adds ½ teaspoon sugar for added flavor as the soup is cooking.)

You can serve this chicken soup with all the vegetables and chicken in it, or strain and serve as a clear broth.

MAKES ABOUT 3 QUARTS

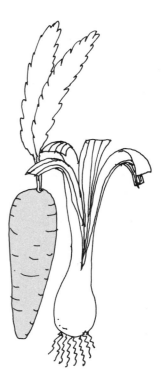

Children love filling out the meal plan in the hospital. Why not create a form for your child, offering nutritious and comforting choices, as well as an occasional treat.

MOM'S CHICKEN SOUP

1 chicken, cut up and cleaned
1 bunch carrots without tops, peeled
    and cut up
1 leek, well washed and cut up
1 onion, chopped
1 bunch celery, washed and coarsely
    chopped (optional)
2 cubes Knorr chicken bouillon
Salt to taste
1 bunch fresh dill

Put everything except the salt and the dill into a stockpot. Cover with cold water (about 3 quarts). Bring to a boil. Reduce the heat and add salt to taste.

Cook, covered, until the chicken is tender, about 2 hours. Add the dill and simmer a few more minutes. Discard the dill.

Strain and de-fat the broth. Serve the broth with chicken and vegetables in individual bowls.

SERVES 4 TO 6

To keep parsley fresh, keep the stems in water, like a bouquet of flowers.

NANA'S CHICKEN SOUP

1 whole chicken
Kosher salt
1 onion
1 carrot
1 stalk celery
1 bay leaf
2 cups cooked rice
Pepper to taste
4 to 5 carrots, peeled and cut up
2 to 3 stalks celery without tops,
    washed and chopped
Fresh parsley, chopped

Remove the giblets and extra fat from the chicken. Wash the chicken thoroughly inside and out. Put in a stockpot and add cold water to cover (about 3 quarts), a tablespoon or two of Kosher salt, and the onion. Bring to a boil, skim off the scum, and add the whole carrot, celery, and bay leaf. Simmer for 2 to 3 hours.

Remove the chicken (which we eat separately with salt). Strain the soup, pushing the cooked carrot, celery, and onion against the strainer to squeeze some of the vegetable juice into the stock. Discard the stock vegetables and add the cooked rice.

Correct the seasoning. Add the cut-up carrots, celery, and parsley and simmer until the vegetables are done, about 15 to 20 minutes.

MAKES ABOUT 3 QUARTS

EGG DROP SOUP

1 (14½-ounce) can chicken broth
½ teaspoon dried dill
½ teaspoon chopped fresh parsley
1 egg
1 teaspoon cold water

Simmer the chicken broth with the dill and parsley. Beat the egg with the cold water until well blended. Add 3 tablespoons of the hot soup to the beaten egg, one at a time. Now pour the egg mixture into the soup. It will form egg drops. You can serve with chow mein noodles.

MAKES ABOUT 2 CUPS

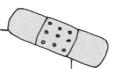

GRANDMA ESSIE'S POTATO SOUP

This soup is chunky—it's really a meal in itself, but if you and the kids like creamy soups, put the soup into the blender or the food processor, two cups at a time, and blend well. It will turn into the best cream of potato soup you've ever had.

3 tablespoons margarine
3 onions, sliced
6 potatoes, peeled and quartered
½ cup sliced carrot
½ cup chopped celery
½ cup chopped green bell pepper
½ cup chopped fresh parsley
½ cup tomato sauce
2 quarts water
1 teaspoon salt
1 tablespoon chopped fresh dill
½ cup margarine
½ cup all-purpose flour

In a large kettle, melt the 3 tablespoons margarine and sauté the onions over low heat until they are very brown. Now add the potatoes, carrot, celery, bell pepper, parsley, tomato sauce, water, and salt. Bring to a boil, lower the heat, and simmer, covered, for about 45 minutes. Add the dill.

In a small saucepan, melt the ½ cup margarine. Add the flour and stir until the flour is brown. Gradually add 1 cup of the soup to the flour mixture, stirring all the time, then add the flour mixture to the remaining soup.

Cook the soup until it thickens and bubbles. Add seasoning to taste.

MAKES 2½ TO 3 QUARTS

PIONEER BREAD

1 small round French bread loaf for each serving
1 recipe Grandma Essie's Potato Soup (above)

Preheat the oven to 250°F.

Cut off the top of each loaf of French bread—hollow out the bottom of each loaf and fill it with potato soup (the soft bread can be reserved for bread crumbs). Put the lid back on and wrap the loaf in aluminum foil. Bake for 1 hour; cool for 10 minutes. When ready to eat, take off the lid. You can tear the lid into pieces that can be dipped into the soup.

MEAT LOAF BURGERS

2 pounds lean ground sirloin
4 tablespoons mayonnaise
4 eggs
½ cup minced green bell pepper
½ cup minced onion
16 large pimiento-stuffed green olives, chopped
2 cups shredded sharp Cheddar cheese
2 large tomatoes, diced
1½ cups chopped white mushrooms
1½ cups chopped soaked dried mushrooms
4 tablespoons wheat germ
¼ teaspoon garlic powder
Salt and pepper to taste
Oil for frying

Combine the meat, mayonnaise, eggs, bell pepper, onion, olives, cheese, tomatoes, mushrooms, wheat germ, garlic powder, and salt and pepper. Mix together and form the mixture into eight patties, each about 1 inch thick. Sauté in a small amount of oil. Cook to the desired doneness.

SERVES 8

ROAST CHICKEN

1 chicken, cut up and cleaned
4 tablespoons olive oil
2 tablespoons melted margarine
1 large head fresh garlic, cut crosswise
*   through the center*
4 sprigs fresh rosemary or
*   1 teaspoon dried*
6 sprigs fresh thyme or
*   1 teaspoon dried*
2 teaspoons red wine vinegar
1 cup canned chicken broth
Salt and pepper to taste
2 tablespoons butter
Fresh thyme sprigs, for garnish

Put the chicken pieces in a large bowl and add the olive oil, melted margarine, garlic, rosemary, and half the thyme sprigs. Cover and refrigerate. Let stand, stirring occasionally, overnight. When ready to cook, scrape the herbs from the chicken.

Preheat the oven to 450°F.

Heat a heavy ovenproof skillet. Place the chicken pieces in one layer. Cook until the chicken is browned, about 4 to 5 minutes. Turn the chicken on the other side and cook until nicely browned, an additional 4 to 5 minutes.

Place the skillet in the oven and bake, uncovered, for 30 minutes. Remove the chicken from the skillet and pour off the fat. Add the vinegar, the broth, the three remaining thyme sprigs tied in a small bundle, and salt and pepper to taste. Bring to a boil on top of the stove and cook about 2 minutes over high heat. Swirl in the butter, stirring, and add any liquid that may flow from the reserved chicken pieces.

Remove the skin from the chicken pieces and arrange the pieces on a serving dish. Garnish with thyme sprigs. Spoon the sauce over and serve.

TUNA CONES

1 (9¼-ounce) can tuna packed in
*   water, drained*
1 stalk celery, washed and chopped
2 tablespoons chopped onion
1 tablespoon relish
2 tablespoons mayonnaise
1 teaspoon lemon juice
Salt and pepper to taste
½ head lettuce, shredded
Flat-bottomed ice-cream cones

Combine all the ingredients except the lettuce and the cones. Chill. Place a handful of lettuce in each cone before serving. Put a scoop of tuna salad on the lettuce in a mound.

SERVES 4

ANGEL HAIR PANCAKES

8 ounces uncooked angel hair noodles
Salt
2 eggs, lightly beaten
Pepper
Melted butter
Sour cream
Fresh dill
Fresh chives (optional)

Boil the noodles in salted water for 1 minute. Drain. Mix the noodles, eggs, salt, and pepper. Spoon small mounds of the mixture onto a hot griddle or skillet coated with melted butter. Cook until brown on both sides. Serve immediately topped with sour cream and dill. If a stronger flavor is desired, add chopped dill and/or chives to taste to the noodle mixture.

SERVES 4 TO 6

CONSOMMÉ RICE

4 tablespoons butter
2 cups white rice
1 cup broken spaghetti (4- to 6-inch pieces)
2 (10½-ounce) cans beef consommé
2 scallions, chopped, or chopped fresh chives, for garnish

Preheat the oven to 375°F.

Melt the butter in a 2-quart ovenproof saucepan. Add the uncooked rice and spaghetti and stir until brown. Add the consommé and cook, covered, for 45 minutes in the oven. Garnish with the chopped scallions.

SERVES 6

NOODLE PUDDING (KUGEL)

1 pound medium flat egg noodles, cooked and drained
6 eggs
1 cup sugar; 5 tablespoons reserved
1 cup melted butter; 5 tablespoons reserved
1 pint sour cream
12 ounces (1½ large packages) cream cheese, softened
1 tablespoon lemon juice
1 teaspoon grated lemon zest
2 cups corn flakes

Preheat the oven to 350°F. Grease a 9-by-12-inch glass baking dish.

In a large mixing bowl, combine the noodles, eggs, sugar (except 5 tablespoons), butter (except 5 tablespoons), sour cream, cream cheese, lemon juice, and lemon zest. Place in the prepared baking dish and refrigerate for 1 hour or overnight.

When ready to bake, combine the corn flakes with the reserved sugar and butter and sprinkle this mixture over the cold kugel. Bake for 1½ hours and serve hot.

BLINTZ CASSEROLE

¼ cup butter or margarine
1 package of 6 frozen blintzes (any kind)
1 cup sour cream
1 teaspoon vanilla extract
4 eggs
¼ cup sugar

Preheat the oven to 350°F.

Melt the butter in a baking dish in the oven. Put in the frozen blintzes. Mix the remaining ingredients and pour over the blintzes. Bake for 1 hour.

Serve with applesauce or other fruit sauce, honey, or maple syrup.

SERVES 2 TO 6, DEPENDING ON APPETITE

CHEESE SOUFFLÉ

3 tablespoons butter
3 tablespoons bread flour
1 cup milk
8 ounces Cheddar or Swiss cheese, grated
6 egg yolks
½ teaspoon Worcestershire sauce
Dash of cayenne pepper
6 egg whites
½ teaspoon salt

Melt the butter in a saucepan and stir in the bread flour. Add the milk. Stir well and cook until thick. Add the cheese. Allow this mixture to cool.

Preheat the oven to 350°F.

Beat the egg yolks, Worcestershire sauce, and cayenne into the cooled cheese mixture. In a separate bowl, whip the egg whites and the salt until very stiff.

Take one-third of the egg whites and fold into the cheese mixture, then add the mixture to the rest of the beaten whites. Fold it in gently, just enough to combine. Turn the mixture into an ungreased baking dish and bake for about 45 minutes or until a knife comes out clean.

SERVES 4

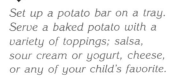

❤

Set up a potato bar on a tray. Serve a baked potato with a variety of toppings; salsa, sour cream or yogurt, cheese, or any of your child's favorite.

FAVORITE MACARONI AND CHEESE

8 ounces macaroni
1 teaspoon butter
1 egg, beaten
1 teaspoon dry mustard
1 teaspoon salt
1 cup milk
3 cups grated sharp cheese

Cook the macaroni according to the package directions; drain thoroughly.

Preheat the oven to 350°F. Butter a 9-by-11-inch casserole dish.

Stir the butter and the egg in with the macaroni. Mix the mustard and the salt with 1 tablespoon hot water and add to the macaroni mixture. Add the milk. Add the cheese, reserving enough to sprinkle on top. Pour the macaroni and cheese mixture into the prepared casserole dish and sprinkle with the reserved cheese. Bake for 45 minutes or until the custard is set and the top is crusty.

SERVES 2 TO 4

❤

For a quick baked potato, use your microwave oven. Prick your potato with a fork, set your microwave on high, and cook for 10 minutes or until tender.

BAKED POTATO

1 medium-size russet potato, well cleaned

Preheat the oven to 400°F.

Pierce the skin of the potato. Bake for 1 hour or until tender.

Try topping your baked potato with plain low-fat yogurt and chives, broccoli and Swiss cheese, Cheddar cheese and bacon, or a combination of your favorite cheeses.

MOM'S CREAM CHEESE POTATOES

9 large russet potatoes, peeled and halved
Salt
2 (3-ounce) packages cream cheese
1 cup sour cream
2 teaspoons onion salt
½ teaspoon pepper
3 tablespoons margarine

Cook the potatoes in boiling salted water until tender. Mash them until smooth. Add the remaining ingredients. Beat with an electric mixer until light and fluffy.

SERVES 8

YAM AND APPLE CASSEROLE

2 pounds yams or sweet potatoes
½ cup melted butter
⅓ cup plus 2 tablespoons light brown sugar
¼ teaspoon salt
½ cup dark corn syrup
1 teaspoon gound cinnamon
2 Granny Smith apples, peeled, cored, and sliced

Cook the yams until tender. Let the yams cool until they can be handled and peel.

Preheat the oven to 350°F. Grease a 9-inch baking dish.

In a food processor or a blender, purée the yams, 5 tablespoons of the melted butter, and the sugar, salt, corn syrup, and cinnamon. Spread half of the puréed mixture in the prepared dish. Layer half of the sliced apples over the purée. Repeat both layers. Brush the top layer of the apples with the remaining 3 tablespoons melted butter. Bake for 30 minutes.

You may assemble, cover, and refrigerate the casserole ahead of time. Bring to room temperature before baking.

SERVES 8

WHIPPED SWEET POTATOES

4 medium sweet potatoes or yams
½ cup butter, softened
2 tablespoons brown sugar
Freshly grated nutmeg

Place the potatoes in a saucepan. Pour in boiling water to cover, and cook for approximately 30 minutes or until the potatoes are cooked through. Drain and allow to cool enough to peel.

Preheat the oven to 300°F.

Peel and mash the potatoes. Add the softened butter. Whip the mixture by hand or with an electric mixer until light and smooth.

Spoon into a heated casserole. Sprinkle the brown sugar and the nutmeg over the top. Place the casserole in the oven to heat the potatoes through (about 10 minutes). Serve hot.

SERVES 4

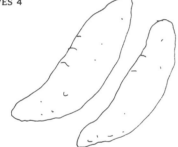

MASHED POTATOES

6 to 8 russet potatoes
¼ cup margarine
Approximately ½ cup warm milk
Salt and pepper to taste

Peel and quarter the potatoes. Place in cold water to prevent them from browning. Drain. Place in a pot with water to cover and bring to a boil. Lower the heat and simmer, covered, for 20 minutes or until the potatoes are very soft and begin to fall apart. Remove from the heat and drain well.

Beat the drained potatoes with an electric mixer. Add the remaining ingredients and beat until quite fluffy and smooth. Serve immediately as is or with butter.

SERVES 4 TO 6

OLD COUNTRY HASH

1¼ pounds baking potatoes, peeled
Salt
1 cup fresh whole wheat bread crumbs
3 tablespoons olive oil
½ cup plus 2 tablespoons grated Parmesan cheese
6 ounces mozzarella cheese, in small cubes
2 eggs, lightly beaten
4 tablespoons chopped fresh parsley
1 clove garlic, minced
¼ teaspoon dried thyme
Pepper to taste
2 tablespoons vegetable oil
2 tablespoons butter or margarine

Cut the potatoes into small cubes and soak in cold water. Drain. Cook in boiling salted water until barely tender, about 5 minutes. Drain and cool in cold water. Drain again and dry with paper towels. Place in a large bowl.

Sauté ½ cup of the bread crumbs in the olive oil. Stir until brown. Combine the sautéed crumbs, ½ cup of the Parmesan cheese, the mozzarella cheese, the eggs, 2 tablespoons of the parsley, the garlic, the thyme, and pepper to taste. Mix with the potatoes.

In an 8- to 9-inch skillet with a flame-proof handle, heat the vegetable oil, coating the sides of the pan. Press the potato mixture firmly into the skillet to form an even layer. Cook over medium heat until the bottom is browned. Remove the pan from the heat. Sprinkle the potato mixture with the remaining ½ cup crumbs, 1 tablespoon parsley, and 2 tablespoons Parmesan cheese. Dot with the butter. Place the pan under the broiler until the top is browned. Run a knife around the edge of the pan to loosen the potatoes.

Garnish with the remaining tablespoon of parsley.

The hash may be prepared ahead of time. Brown under the broiler, cool in the pan, and refrigerate. To reheat, place in a preheated 350°F oven for 10 to 15 minutes or until heated through.

SERVES 7 TO 8

♥
Joni Staigers uses bags of frozen peas or corn niblets for cold compresses because, she says, "they mold to whatever part of the body needs the cold." Frozen vegetables can also be eaten out of the bag as a treat.

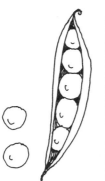

EMERALD ISLE PURÉE

1 package frozen lima beans
1 (6-ounce) can small peas
1½ tablespoons heavy cream or half-and-half (optional)
Salt and white pepper to taste
½ teaspoon ground nutmeg
1 tablespoon butter

Cook the lima beans according to the package directions. Warm the peas in their own juice. Drain the beans and the peas, reserving some of the liquid. Combine both in a food processor or a blender. Add either the cream or some of the leftover cooking liquid and purée to a smooth consistency. Salt and pepper to taste. Put in a 2-quart serving dish. Sprinkle with nutmeg. Dot the top with pats of the butter.

SERVES 4

DESSERTS

APPLE CRISP

1 cup rolled oats
1 cup all-purpose flour
1 cup brown sugar
1 cup sugar
1 cup butter, softened
1 teaspoon ground cinnamon
½ teaspoon ground nutmeg
6 to 8 large apples, peeled, cored, and sliced

Preheat the oven to 350°F. Grease a 9-by-13-inch pan.
Combine the oats, flour, sugars, butter, cinnamon, and nutmeg. Blend the mixture together until crumbly. Place the apple slices in the prepared pan and top with the oat mixture. Bake for 40 minutes or until the topping is crunchy and brown.

SERVES 8 TO 10

♥
Apple Crisp and rice pudding make a delicious and healthy breakfast. Try them with a cup of hot tea.

CHEESECAKE
Crust

¾ cup finely crumbled graham crackers
2 tablespoons sugar
½ teaspoon ground cinnamon
6 tablespoons melted butter or margarine
2 tablespoons butter, softened

Filling

3 (8-ounce) packages cream cheese, softened
1¼ cups sugar
6 egg yolks
1 pint sour cream
3 tablespoons all-purpose flour
2 teaspoons vanilla extract
1 tablespoon lemon juice
1 tablespoon finely grated lemon zest
6 egg whites
2 tablespoons powdered sugar

Prepare the crust: Combine the graham cracker crumbs, sugar, and cinnamon in a mixing bowl. Stir the melted butter into the cracker crumbs until they are well saturated. Butter a 9-by-3-inch springform pan with the 2 tablespoons soft butter. Pat an even layer of the cracker crumb mixture on the bottom and sides of the pan with your fingers to form a shell. Refrigerate while you make the filling.
Preheat the oven to 350°F.
Cream the softened cheese by beating it with a spoon in a mixing bowl until it is smooth. Beat in the sugar gradually. Beat in the egg yolks one at a time. Continue to beat until all the ingredients are combined. Stir in the sour cream, flour, vanilla, lemon juice, and zest.
Beat the egg whites until they are stiff enough to form peaks when the beaters are lifted out of the bowl. Fold the egg whites gently but thoroughly into the cream cheese mixture until no streaks of white show. Do not overfold.
Pour the filling into the prepared pan. Spread it evenly. Bake in the middle of the oven for 1 hour. Turn off the oven and let the cake rest on the oven shelf for 15 min-

utes, leaving the oven door open. Remove the cheesecake from the oven and allow to cool to room temperature. Remove the sides of the pan and sprinkle the cake with powdered sugar before serving.

SERVES 8

CHOCOLATE BREAD PUDDING

10 slices white bread, crusts removed
1½ cups sugar
2 ounces (2 squares) unsweetened chocolate
1½ cups milk
2 eggs
¼ teaspoon vanilla extract

In a food processor or a blender, process the bread until it is coarse, lumpy crumbs. There should be 4 cups. Combine the crumbs with the sugar in a mixing bowl.

In a saucepan over low heat, melt the chocolate in the milk. Do not bring to a boil. Allow to cool and pour into the food processor or the blender. Blend with the eggs. Pour the mixture into the top of a double boiler. Add the bread crumb–sugar mixture. Blend well. Cook, uncovered, over low heat for 45 minutes. Stir occasionally. Add the vanilla. Serve warm topped with crème fraîche or whipped cream.

SERVES 8

PORCUPINES

1 tablespoon melted butter
½ cup sugar
1 egg
Pinch of salt
1 cup chopped unsweetened dates
1 cup chopped nuts
1 teaspoon vanilla extract
2 cups shredded coconut

Preheat the oven to 350°F.
Combine all the ingredients except the shredded coconut. Roll the mixture into logs 2 inches long, then roll in the coconut. Bake for 15 to 20 minutes.

MAKES APPROXIMATELY 2 DOZEN

RICE PUDDING

3 eggs
2 cups cooked brown rice
3 cups milk (whole, low-fat, or skim)
¼ cup brown sugar
1 cup raisins
½ teaspoon mixed ground cinnamon and ground nutmeg

Preheat the oven to 325°F. Grease a square casserole.

In a large bowl, beat the eggs. Add all the other ingredients to the eggs and mix well. Pour into the prepared dish. Bake for about 1 hour or until set. Serve the pudding hot or cold.

SERVES 6

LEMON ICE

3½ cups water
1¼ cups sugar
¾ cup fresh lemon juice
2 tablespoons lemon zest
6 sprigs fresh mint

Boil the water in a saucepan. Stir the sugar into the boiling water until dissolved. Remove from the heat and cool. Add the lemon juice and zest. Pour the mixture into a metal bowl. Freeze. When ready to serve, beat the ice until fluffy, scoop, and serve. Top each serving with a mint sprig.

SERVES 6

Raspberry, strawberry, pineapple, cranberry, or orange juice make delicious ices as well. Remember to decrease the amount of sugar.

154

LEMON SQUARES

2 cups all-purpose flour
½ cup powdered sugar, plus extra for
    dusting
1 cup melted unsalted butter
2 large lemons
2 cups sugar
1 tablespoon melted unsalted butter
4 large eggs

Preheat the oven to 350°F.
Sift together the flour and the powdered sugar in a medium bowl. Add the melted butter and mix with your hands to form a dough. Press the dough into an 8-by-8-inch baking pan until flat and even. Bake for 15 minutes.

While the shortbread is baking, prepare the lemon curd. Carefully grate the zest from the lemons; be careful not to include any of the bitter white pith. Squeeze the juice from the lemons and set aside. In a medium bowl, whisk together the sugar, butter, eggs, lemon juice, and zest. When the shortbread has baked for 15 minutes, pour the lemon mixture over it and level with a spatula.

Bake for 20 to 25 minutes, until the curd is set. Dust with sifted powdered sugar. Cool and cut into squares.

MAKES 16 (2-INCH) SQUARES

WHIPPED GELATIN

1 (3.4-ounce) package strawberry-
    or raspberry-flavored gelatin
⅓ cup whipped cream, sour cream,
    or yogurt
1 mashed banana
Coarsely chopped pecans or walnuts

Make the gelatin with 2 cups hot water and refrigerate until fairly well set.

Place the gelatin, cream, and mashed banana in a food processor and mix until well blended. Add the nuts. Remove to a bowl and refrigerate until well set. Serve in individual bowls.

SERVES 4

CHOCOLATE CHOW MEIN NOODLE COOKIES

Susan Diamond's best invention is these popular cookies.

12 ounces semisweet chocolate chips
1 (5-ounce) can chow mein noodles
1 cup unsalted peanuts

Melt the chocolate chips in the microwave oven or the top of a double boiler. Pour the chocolate into a bowl and add the noodles and the nuts. Drop by large teaspoonfuls onto waxed paper and allow to set. Transfer to a serving dish. Enjoy!

MAKES APPROXIMATELY 2 DOZEN COOKIES

CHOCOLATE CHIPS

QUICK TAPIOCA CUSTARD

3 tablespoons quick-cooking tapioca
½ cup sugar
¼ teaspoon salt
1 or 2 beaten eggs
2 cups milk
½ teaspoon vanilla extract (optional)
1 teaspoon grated orange or
    lemon zest (optional)

Combine all the ingredients except the vanilla and grated zest in the top of a double boiler. Stir. Cook over rapidly boiling water for 7 minutes without stirring. Stir and cook 5 minutes longer. Remove the top part of the double boiler and set aside; the tapioca will thicken as it cools. For a light custard, separate the eggs and add one stiffly beaten egg white after the tapioca cools. Fold in the vanilla or the grated orange or lemon zest gradually. Chill.

SERVES 4

GRANOLA COOKIES

Remy Weber's all-time favorites.

½ cup butter or margarine, softened
½ cup sugar
½ cup brown sugar
1 egg
1 teaspoon vanilla extract
1 cup all-purpose flour
¼ teaspoon baking soda
½ teaspoon baking powder
1 cup rolled oats
1 cup shredded unsweetened coconut
½ cup sunflower seeds
¼ cup sesame seeds
1 cup flake cereal like corn flakes or
    Wheaties
1 cup raisins

Preheat the oven to 350°F.
Cream the butter with the sugars. Add the egg and the vanilla. Add the remaining ingredients and mix well. Spoon by dollops onto a cookie sheet and bake for about 10 minutes.

MAKES ABOUT 2 DOZEN COOKIES

WACKY CAKE

1½ cups sifted all-purpose flour
1 cup sugar
1 tablespoon cocoa powder
1 teaspoon baking soda
½ teaspoon salt
1 tablespoon vinegar
1 teaspoon vanilla extract
6 tablespoons vegetable oil

Preheat the oven to 350°F.
Sift all the dry ingredients into an 8-by-8-inch pan. (No need to use a mixing bowl.) Make three wells in the dry ingredients and pour the vinegar into one hole, the vanilla into the next, and the vegetable oil into the third. Pour 1 cup of water over the entire pan. Stir until all the lumps are out. Bake for 25 to 30 minutes.

Frosting

2 cups powdered sugar
4 tablespoons butter, softened
1 teaspoon vanilla extract
2 tablespoons milk

Mix all the ingredients until spreadable and spread on the cooked cake.

SERVES 8 TO 10

GOLDINE'S BROWNIES

½ cup butter or margarine
2 ounces (2 squares) unsweetened
    chocolate
1 cup sugar
¾ cup broken pecans
⅔ cup self-rising flour
1 teaspoon vanilla extract
2 eggs

Preheat the oven to 350°F.
Grease the bottom of an 8-inch square pan. Melt the butter and the chocolate in a saucepan. Remove from the heat. Add all the remaining ingredients except the eggs. Stir to mix well. Add the eggs and beat well. Bake for approximately 30 minutes. Cool. Cut into squares and store covered.

MAKES APPROXIMATELY 16 (2-INCH) SQUARES

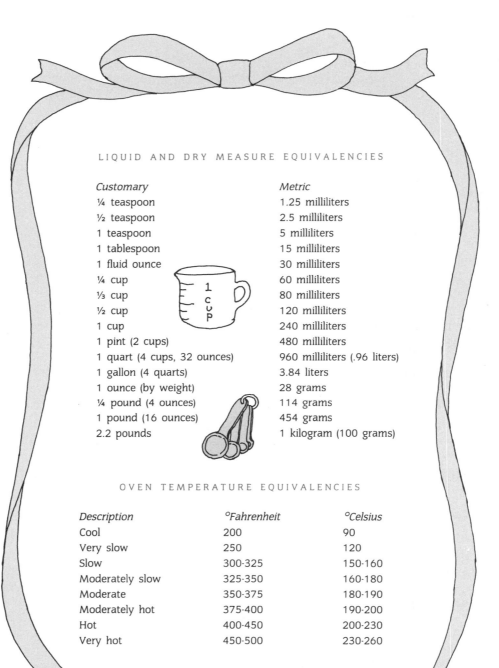

LIQUID AND DRY MEASURE EQUIVALENCIES

Customary	Metric
¼ teaspoon	1.25 milliliters
½ teaspoon	2.5 milliliters
1 teaspoon	5 milliliters
1 tablespoon	15 milliliters
1 fluid ounce	30 milliliters
¼ cup	60 milliliters
⅓ cup	80 milliliters
½ cup	120 milliliters
1 cup	240 milliliters
1 pint (2 cups)	480 milliliters
1 quart (4 cups, 32 ounces)	960 milliliters (.96 liters)
1 gallon (4 quarts)	3.84 liters
1 ounce (by weight)	28 grams
¼ pound (4 ounces)	114 grams
1 pound (16 ounces)	454 grams
2.2 pounds	1 kilogram (100 grams)

OVEN TEMPERATURE EQUIVALENCIES

Description	°Fahrenheit	°Celsius
Cool	200	90
Very slow	250	120
Slow	300-325	150-160
Moderately slow	325-350	160-180
Moderate	350-375	180-190
Moderately hot	375-400	190-200
Hot	400-450	200-230
Very hot	450-500	230-260

♥ Parental Consent Form for Medical Care ♥

TO WHOM IT MAY CONCERN:

(We) (I) hereby grant permission to _____ to
secure such medical care as _____ may require
for period from _____ to _____ , including
examination, treatment, and immunization. This permission is conditional upon
the understanding that in the event of serious illness or the need for operation
and/or major surgery, _____ , guardian, will
use all reasonable efforts to contact me. Failure in such efforts, however,
should not prevent _____ , guardian, from providing
such emergency treatment as may be necessary for his/her best interest.

_____
SIGNATURE

_____
SIGNATURE

FAMILY DOCTOR

_____
Address

_____
Phone

(FOR EACH CHILD)